ARCHITECTURE: THE DESIGN EXPERIENCE

HUGH STUBBINS

ARCHITECTURE: THE DESIGN EXPERIENCE

Editing by SUSAN BRAYBROOKE
Book Design by HUGH STUBBINS
and MERLE WESTLAKE

Foreword by MARCEL BREUER
Introduction by MILDRED SCHMERTZ

A WILEY-INTERSCIENCE PUBLICATION

JOHN WILEY & SONS

New York • London • Sydney • Toronto

Quotations on pages 6 and 75 are taken from the following sources:

Jonathan Barnett, *Urban Design as Public Policy,* Architectural Record Books, McGraw-Hill, Inc., New York, 1974, by permission of the publisher.

Ray Faulkner and Edwin Ziegfeld, *Art Today,* Holt, Rinehart, and Winston, Inc., New York, 1969, pp. 11 and 12, by permission of the publisher.

Library of Congress Cataloging in Publication Data:

Stubbins, Hugh, 1912–
  Architecture, the design experience.

  "A Wiley-Interscience publication."
  Includes index.
  1. Architectural design. 2. Hugh Stubbins and Associates. 3. Architecture, Modern—20th century—United States—Case studies. I. Title.

NA2750.S88   720'.6'57444   75-42173
ISBN 0-471-83482-3

Printed in the United States of American

10 9 8 7 6 5 4 3 2 1

For my friends and colleagues of
Hugh Stubbins and Associates
who shared the design experience
and without whom there would be
no architecture to write about.

Foreword

The work of Hugh Stubbins is an impressive line of positive statements, an unusual interreaction of responsibility and talent. While he is circumspect and alert, responsive to new ideas, whether produced by technology or by the dreams of changing history, he recognizes and uses his own resources with a sure and consistent hand.

I met him more than 30 years ago, in the faculty of the Harvard School of Design. What impressed me from the start was his lean youthfulness, his working capacity, and his levelheaded modesty, helped along considerably by a slight southern accent—for which my weakness is incurable. At that time, the middle of the forties, his main interest was the house in the country, the frame house—the beginning of his career, which carried him, in a logical, continuous development, a long distance from there. These houses—so-called modern architecture, had a distinctly American flavor. One felt the native forest, even if there was not a tree around. One felt as though they were surrounded by great distances, large spaces, even if, in fact, they were part of a close settlement. They employ materials and building methods that can be changed and adjusted to new needs, not necessarily by an expert, but by practically anyone. His "homemade" materials even when approaching the primitive, fulfill their purpose in a most sophisticated way.

Stubbins' work gives a special significance to the details. The monumental conception of his later projects never lets him forget that technical and useful solutions of the parts are the ones nearest to our skin, our eyes, and our hands.

MARCEL BREUER

Preface

Why should an architect write a book? For the glory and conceit of it? I have to admit my motives are not entirely pure. After nearly 35 years in practice, I confess a desire a consider my work in sum, to bind it between covers and see it take its place among the handsome volumes produced by many of my peers.

When buildings are completed and occupied, they take on a life of their own and the design process is quickly forgotten. A book provides a permanent record of the context of the design experience.

But there is something more. There are things I want to say to architects about architecture, and to the client and user group, some things I want to say about architects.

There has never been a greater need for architectural services, and yet there has probably never been less understanding of the services architects can and should provide. Architects do not understand themselves very well, and the general public understands them hardly at all.

This book is an attempt to bridge that gap, to get inside the process and sort out the forces that converge to make a building. In subjecting my work to this kind of scrutiny, I have learned some hard lessons. I have been forced to look closely at the day-to-day working of my office, to examine processes hitherto taken for granted, to analyze relationships in terms of their creativity or lack of it, to evaluate buildings—not just as solutions to specific problems—but as expressions of professional development in an increasingly complex age.

In the past few years, architecture has gained much greater social and political content. The involvement of the community in the design process has become one of today's preoccupations—as has the team approach to design. But the questions remain—what does such involvement do to architecture or to the design process? Is architectural technology a social contract or an art? Does it matter if the profession as such survives?

As a profession, we must answer our critics by asking these questions of ourselves, by examining our professional stance and procedures and the educational philosophy on which they are based. For it is only by broadening and deepening our intellectual base that we can hope to move forward to provide the kind of service that the public demands of us and, in the final analysis, that we demand of ourselves.

Many people have helped me with this book and I am grateful to them all. Dudley Hunt (with his colleagues at John Wiley in New York) has been a patient, understanding, and always wise editor. The late William B. Foxhall gave me perceptive counsel in the conceptual stage. To my chief collaborators Susan Braybrooke and Merle Westlake I owe special thanks for a team effort which was at all times enjoyable.

HUGH STUBBINS

Cambridge, Massachusetts
January 1976

CONTENTS

Introduction

Why should Hugh Stubbins write a book? He is not a theorist nor a polemicist. He never founded a style or joined an aesthetic movement, nor did he ever, even when young, write a manifesto. In 35 years of active and successful practice he has been glad to leave the task of architectural interpretation to the critics and historians. Many of them, in their understandable preoccupation with movements, isms, form giving, name making, and stars, have paid too little attention to him.

Some of the best architects of every generation have produced work impossible to classify in terms of style. Stubbins is one of a small number of first-rate architects in the United States whose work eludes the systematized or not so systematized categorizations of those who are today interpreting architecture within a historic and cultural framework. One can, however, predict that the work of Stubbins and his several peers will one day be seen for what it is—a post–World War II contemporary vernacular designed at a level of seriousness, honesty, modesty, and humaneness not seen in U.S. architecture since the mid-nineteenth century. This vernacular, at its strongest and most consistent in New England, is largely made up of nonmonumental buildings for everyday practical human use—houses and housing, schools, college buildings, and libraries. Stubbins' contribution to this body of work has been significant, even though it does not constitute his entire output, and for this reason alone, it is historically important that he select his best completed buildings and projects and put them all together as he has done in this book.

Architecture, in the end, is what gets built. The architecture of an era is a collection of buildings, not a mass of theory. Successful architects have always been pragmatists, fighting and compromising in the tough everyday world to get their buildings up and finished.

Stubbins is a practical architect, pragmatic in the better sense of that double-edged word. For him architectural thought must lead to the act of building, architectural concepts must be examined in the light of the possible, and the validity of a design idea must be tested in terms of its consequences for those who believe it to be appropriate and for everybody else who may be affected by it.

According to engineer William LeMessurier, who has worked with him on many projects, Stubbins is a good architect by all the measures of professional performance. His buildings are beautiful and they work. He is a good site planner. He meets deadlines and budgets. He understands how to make the best use of consultants. He has built a well-balanced team of staff and associates. His office is a good—and for many a happy—place to work. "Most importantly," says LeMessurier, "he wins the trust of good clients and keeps it. They begin by respecting him as a businessman and come to know and regard him as an artist."

If an architect is to be more than a theorist and polemicist, he must get work. Architects whose thinking is too far in advance of their own time seldom find clients. Although their influence may be kept alive in books and journals, their long-range effectiveness will diminish. Unfortunately, the details but not the essence of their few built projects are often copied in weaker versions by more fortunate architects who do get commissions. Very often the aesthetic borrowings are inappropriate to the task at hand.

Because Stubbins is a fine designer in his own right, in addition to being a good businessman and job getter, he doesn't lose his way in the maze of contemporary and historic styles available to today's architect. Unlike some of the followers of Wright, Stubbins has not romantically borrowed and transformed the shapes of nature in ways that deny our existence in a technological society and pretend to a pastoral world. So far he has avoided pure Mies; the decorated International Style of Stone and Yamasaki; the inclusionist, eclectic palettes of Kahn, Venturi, and Moore; and the exclusionist pieties of the Corbu Revivalists.

Stubbins does, however, acknowledge the influence upon his development of his pre-Harvard training at Georgia Institute of Technology from 1928 to 1933, during which time the architectural school still issued design problems prepared by the Beaux Arts Institute. His design critics were the leading practitioners of Atlanta, and he remembers this school as a very good place. Each Beaux Arts design problem was a small competition with medals handed out by eminent architects in New York. Stubbins admits to having been highly competitive at that time—not only within the Beaux Arts system, but also in other areas of life. (He was once the champion short-distance runner in his state.) When not running, he was learning Beaux Arts rendering techniques: He ground his own Chinese ink, learned to "make a stretch," and ran washes that graded imperceptibly and elegantly from light to dark and cast elaborate shadows. The Beaux Arts system also taught him to analyze a complex program quickly in functional terms and come up with a workable solution. There was never time to change his mind. The design solution did not need to be axially symmetrical in the classic manner as many people think, but it had to satisfy a need for balance and order.

When Stubbins went on to Harvard for graduate work, the Beaux Arts system was still in force there. He received his Master in Architecture degree in 1935—2 years before the arrival of Walter Gropius as chairman of the department brought the beginning of the end of Beaux Arts training in the United States.

Although Stubbins returned to Harvard in 1940 as Gropius' assistant, became an associate professor at the Harvard Graduate School of Design in 1946, and following Gropius' resignation, became chairman of the department in 1953, this long and friendly association with the great architect had an indirect, subtle, but nonstylistic effect on Stubbins' design aesthetic. Gropius' influence was intellectual, philosophical, and idealistic.

On the other hand, Marcel Breuer, who had also taught at Harvard, influenced Stubbins in more discernible ways. Breuer's knowledge of how to place buildings on a site, his grasp of domestic scale, and his uncompromising commitment to technological development and expression are shared by Stubbins. Although today their large-scale work shares little or no expressive similarities, they had much in common at the beginning of Stubbins' career, as can be seen in the early houses and housing projects shown in this book.

In Alvar Aalto, Stubbins has found both teacher and friend. "I first met him when he was designing Baker House at MIT, sometime in the mid-forties. In those days our lunches used to last until 2 A.M. I saw him again most recently in Finland, just a few years ago. We never discuss theory when we meet. The last time, at his house, we just sat around drinking and eating

xiv

a lot of bear meat." Stubbins' use of the relaxed, curving line, as in the garden wall of the Loeb Drama Center at Harvard, is in the manner of Aalto, as is his unfailing attention to silhouette—particularly at the juncture of building to sky, plane to plane, material to material. Like Aalto, Stubbins pays a lot of attention to the scale, color, and texture of the materials he juxtaposes, dramatizing them where appropriate by extreme contrast, as in the Santa Cruz campus at the University of California, or by moderate contrast, as in the Countway Library of Medicine at Harvard.

With regard to influences, however, it should be said that lessons learned from the Beaux Arts, Breuer, and Aalto cannot be more than the most tenuous guidelines to an architect whose work must answer the increasingly complex aesthetic, technical, and social questions of today. Vast urban projects like Citicorp in New York City, the Federal Reserve Bank of Boston, and Spring Venture are without precedent in their complexity. Citicorp, as Stubbins points out in this book, must meet the corporate goals of the First National City Bank in its banking headquarters and provide an office tower, new shops and restaurants, and a community church to replace an old one—all on a tight city block.

Such projects simply cannot be adequately solved by an architect locked within a single crystallized style. Stubbins' book makes it clear why he has always avoided this trap. He returns again and again to the point that architecture is more than the creation of forms and that, indeed, the profession has been seriously hurt by its emphasis on formalistic approaches. On the other hand, Stubbins has never let the practical problems of building overwhelm his aesthetic concerns.

A Stubbins building or urban complex appears to emerge from its program without having been affected by too many preconceptions, either social or aesthetic. His own description of the design process, as revealed in the case studies in this book, indicates that he often sees the planning task within a broader scale of values and concerns than his client may perceive in the beginning. The Countway Library, for example, had to be a monumental building in an already powerful neoclassic setting, and this wider cultural objective was met, along with the more practical program requirements.

Stubbins tries to find the appropriate physical form for each building he designs in terms of its basic purpose, which is usually a combination of practical, social, aesthetic, and psychological objectives. It has been said before that the architects who give the world the most powerful forms do so by electing to solve only a few of the problems posed by a given program. Stubbins, who tries to solve as many of the problems as possible, has been willing to settle for less dramatic shapes. Those who will use his buildings are constantly in his thoughts, and he tries to create an atmosphere that will help them do better and more happily what they do.

Stubbins became an architect because in the devout Presbyterian household in which he grew up in Birmingham, Alabama, it was considered a fine thing for young boys talented at painting and drawing to grow up to be architects (there were several distinguished, gentlemanly architects in town) but a bad thing for them to grow up to be painters and go off to live in Paris. Unless Hugh takes up painting again, we will never know what kind of painter he might have been. But the countless numbers of people who have lived part of their lives in his buildings do, at some level of their consciousness, experience his architecture as good.

MILDRED F. SCHMERTZ

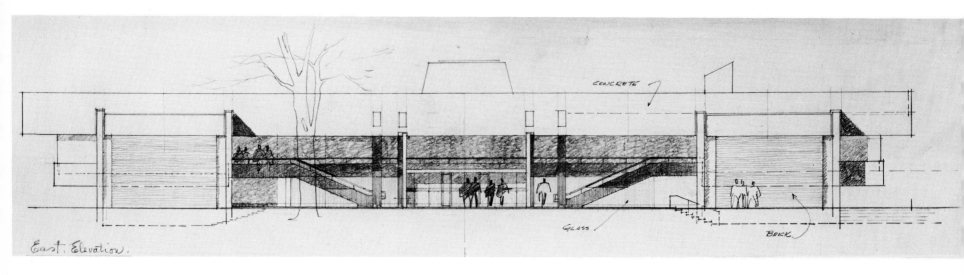

CONCRETE

GLASS

BRICK

East Elevation.

Thoughts on Architecture

ATTITUDES

The architect in the seventies has become something of an anti-hero. From convention floors, professional journals, and within his own strangely masochistic psyche, he finds his vision of the world attacked, his problem-solving techniques branded for unrealism or irrelevance, his solutions assailed for egocentricity or inhumanity. Although no responsible profession can afford to ignore such criticism, in the inevitable overreaction there is a tendency to throw out truth with dogma. Recent criticism notwithstanding, some of the Bauhaus principles were good. There is a place for ascetic beauty in this age of Western overindulgence, a part of the human soul that responds to this disciplined economy, and some need for formalism, rationalism, simplicity and restraint.

criticism and the crisis in confidence

The visionary planning principles of the twenties have been discredited today, and we are preoccupied with man's craving for identity in a technological world. A yearning for homogeneity, a distinctly sentimental attachment to the past, and a preoccupation with the "long littleness of life" have colored our approaches to city planning. Thus, Le Corbusier's *voisin* plan or Soleri's Arcosanti are considered at best fanciful, at worst fascist and technocratic. The futuristic vision of the city is overcome by the need for the corner paper store, the companionship of the stoop, the security of the neighborhood bar.

How can the practicing architect deal with this abrupt reversal of values? Must he abandon the gods of his youth? Must he equate the planner with the planned? What projection of the future can he invoke to modify the program requirements of the present? For he knows that the client group of today is only a tenant of his buildings, and future tenants may be ill served by too slavish an observance of timely decisions, no matter how thoroughly researched.

The philosophical dilemma is difficult for any generation, for the public demands paradoxical qualities from architecture. Criticized for virtuosity and lack of sympathy with human needs, the architect may be equally assailed for the anonymous or impersonal buildings that result from the ultimate priority of flexibility and utility.

Architectural visionaries have fallen into the traps that beset all revolutionaries: oversimplification of ideas, dedication to progress without due consideration of the technological or social content of such change, and a tendency to reduce the diversity of life to universal themes. Yet without the impetus that comes from such vision it is difficult for human beings even to contemplate the possibility of new ways of living and new cultural and social organisms. Resistance to change, the fear of the unknown, the stultifying security of the familiar can keep us forever in a world of mediocrity. Somewhere, in the recognition of both these forces, is the hope for a meaningful future for our man-made environment.

The architectural profession today is in a defensive and confused condition. The architect's influence over the physical environment is still in question. The proportion of new building over which architects have some control is still very low. We see developers, engineers, and builders apparently getting on quite well without us. Our omnipotence has been successively threatened by the computer, by industrialized building, and, in a different way, by the tremendous fluctuations in the economy, with which the structure of architectural practice is not equipped to cope. Untrained as businessmen, unacceptable as pure artists, seemingly unwilling to join the different building teams in anything but a leadership role, we are not sure how to approach our future, and the future is hard to find.

The whole business of architecture has become infinitely more complex since I first started in practice. Projects are larger. Far more agencies and business undertakings, community and special-interest groups are represented in the process. The level of technical complexity is much greater. The clearly definable patron has vanished. The community at large has become our client, and the team is the thing.

Despite the lip service given to teamwork, however, the team approach to architecture is not as well established as one might wish. The fact that many more specialized consultants are now involved on major projects does not in itself guarantee a true team effort, any more than a group of ad hoc athletes constitutes a winning football team. The building team has to be as carefully orchestrated as a symphony. But this orchestration does not always take place. Consultants may be retained at different times in the process—often much too late—with the result that decisions affecting their contribution have already been made before they come aboard. Some consultants may be employed by the architect, others directly by the client, and this can result in unedifying struggles. The operation and success of the team depend on its constitution

and directorship. More thought should be given to this at the outset and should be realistically reflected in budgets and contractual agreements. True interdisciplinary collaboration—essential as it is to the future of architecture—cannot be wished into existence. It requires an understanding of the entire process, trust, confidence, and, above all, hard work, particularly from architects who have been traditionally cast on the conductor's podium.

The business of architecture has often been hard for the individual architect to accept. Commercial success and design integrity are frequently seen as opposing forces whose marriage inevitably involves disagreeable compromise. While the dangers of crass commercialism in the design and construction industry are obvious—and we are all suffering their environmental consequences—we cannot afford to hover forever between art and reality. Attracted to the one, repelled by the other, unable to exist comfortably in either camp, we badly incapacitate ourselves by dwelling in a halfway house.

This tension is reflected in many architectural offices that—for all their avowed commitment to humanity, creativity, and teamwork—are not always the pleasant and stimulating places they purport to be. Possessiveness and competition between creative people over ideas can make for a nervous atmosphere fraught with tension and antithetical to inspired group endeavor. Perhaps there is too little opportunity for architects to change their roles or express their opinions in a constructive atmosphere, and I think there is certainly too little personal and professional recognition for individual contributions to design. Architectural offices must devote time to education as well as to practice, indeed at present they are the main forum for the continuing education of the profession. Too much "classified" information exists in the archives of individual offices. A sincere effort is essential if we are to share our professional experience through professional affiliations, publication of work, and open, informal discussion of problem solving.

The unwillingness to recognize that architecture is indeed a business and that architectural offices need clients, profits, and growth potential for their own health and that of their clients is having disastrous results for the profession. Reluctant to adapt modern business techniques and management methods to our own use, we have suffered much more than is necessary from the fluctuations of the economy.

architecture is a business, but the architect is an untrained businessman

The business of getting new work is fundamental to the continued life of an architectural practice, and—in one way or another—development or promotion accounts for a considerable amount of principals' time, support staff, and overhead expenditure. Yet architects are only now beginning to accept this realistically, allocate time and budget resources to the effort, and deal seriously with the whole question of public relations. Ashamed, perhaps, of the thought of selling their services and unable to advertise, architects are forced to expand and contract their offices drastically as one project ends or the next begins and to suffer the resulting administrative disruption and negative effect on morale.

Planned development and controlled growth—second nature to the businessman—are foreign concepts to many architects. Business does not have to fight this battle. It is clearly recognized that sales and production are both essential parts of the same organization—that one is complementary to the other—and that success can be achieved only with both.

Possibly more devastating than its effect on the internal structure of architectural offices is the negative influence this kind of attitude exerts over the client–architect relationship. The client is in many cases frankly a businessman who finds no reason to apologize for the profit motive, who is committed to a good building nevertheless, and who expects his architect to understand the pressures he is operating under. But do we architects understand? Do we even try to understand? Do we understand the hierarchy of the corporate client, the bureaucracy, the ponderous approval mechanisms? Do we recognize that rentability may take precedence over flexibility and that the client representative may be replaced for too strong and overt a commitment to beauty at the expense of budget? If we cannot understand these things, we cannot work effectively in the framework of our society. We may deplore many of these pressures and restrictions; we may even work with the client to override or circumvent them; but we must know that these forces exist and must believe that good architecture is possible despite them. There is never a single solution.

To architects, and indeed to many people, the real estate entrepreneurs or developers have been thought of as the real villains in the expansions of our communities. We have all seen the bulldozer turn the countryside into a wasteland, have walked through unrelieved acres of "tract" houses, and have driven by strip developments that make American city fringes among the ugliest in the world. In our country public ownership of land is limited, and control of the physical environment is largely in private hands. Like it or not, the real estate industry holds the key to the American environment in the foreseeable future. If we are to influence the shape and character of this environment, we are going to have to learn to work constructively with developers; this may be the most creative challenge facing the profession today.

influencing the environment via the real estate industry

While holding no brief for the ravages wrought by land developers in the past, I believe that today we are dealing with a much more sophisticated profession. They understand and are often sympathetic to conservation, and they have tried harder than architects to understand how America wants to live. Their profit motive is tempered by a pioneering zeal. They are concerned in upgrading the quality of life and want exciting and innovative approaches to planning. If architects cannot offer better solutions, they will find other ways of achieving the goals. So it behooves us to join the development team. It is our chance at this time to add that "plus" to the built environment.

EDUCATION

In 350 years, starting from a wilderness, America has managed to build the world's largest and ugliest cities. If we look around us at all of our man-made world—at our cities—at our suburbs, what do we see? Unfortunately, a great many people look and do not see. If they could see, they would be overwhelmed by the general ugliness of the vast, amorphous display of chaotic structure that surrounds us and is steadily creeping over the countryside. Though many people may not recognize or be able to analyze this ugliness, it takes its toll nonetheless. The monotony of mediocrity typical of so many of our communities dulls the mind, depresses the spirit, and often flattens the pocketbook. Although much of the visual anarchy that assaults us is the by-product of decay and neglect, there is also much ugliness in new developments that have had no time to decay. We are building ugliness in from the beginning.

Buildings are constructed because of the demands of society— whether they be purely utilitarian or symbolic. They are not built for purposes that established society rejects. Few, if any, purposeless buildings have been made. But if we conclude from this that man demands the ugliness he gets, we would be indulging in the cynicism that paralyzes action and denies hope. We would be depriving the architectural profession of any reason for being.

It is to the education of the architect—and especially of the public—that the architectural profession must look for an answer to the creeping blight of our environment. We must ask if the coming generation of architects is being educated to make an effective contribution in a world that seems hardly aware of its existence.

people must be taught to see

In the creation of complex environmental facilities, many disciplines must come into play through the talents of individuals specially trained in them. The resulting building or complex of buildings, to be successful aesthetically, physically, economically, and socially, must be the sum total of these many talents. The result will certainly represent a summation of knowledge beyond the capability of any single individual.

The desired results will not be achieved, unless at the center of the creative planning process there is a man or woman or a small group comprehending the whole effort and able to organize it to achieve the creative vision. All must be trained as specialists in the main trunks of knowledge from which all other branches grow.

a comprehensive vision at the core of successful group endeavor

For this to happen, the schools must increase the scope and depth of their interdisciplinary courses. Architects must learn early to talk to lawyers, work with real estate developers, empathize with community groups, and understand the subtleties of the political process. They must understand the psychology of business communication—the gamesmanship— and must discern the moments when people mean what they say, when they are looking for help, when they want resistance, and when they don't. They have to learn the realities of bargaining and compromise, whether they approve of them or not. As Jonathan Barnett says in his book *Urban Design as Public Policy,* "The day to day decisions about the allocation of government money according to conflicting needs and different political interests, or the economics of real estate investment, are in fact the medium of city design, as essential to the art as paint is to the painter. To produce meaningful results, from both a practical and artistic point of view, urban designers must rid themselves of the notion that their work will be contaminated by an understanding of political and real estate decisions. It is not always necessary to approve; it is essential to understand." Architects, no less than urban designers, must learn how projects come into being and how approval hierarchies work, if they are to influence the decisions made.

need for a new focus on the realities of practice and the politics of decision making

Traditionally, architectural students are taught by architects; their design solutions are criticized by architects; and it is hardly surprising, therefore, if they learn to design for architects. Upon graduation they are often ill equipped to present their work convincingly to clients and ill prepared to deal with the criticism clients may make. In school, the student is presenting his work to the initiated. Many things need no explanation to his tutor but may require considerable clarification for the corporate client or the community group. Although some architects are naturally articulate, most are not, because their natural method of communication is visual. Those who can explain and describe their work logically and convincingly have a tremendous advantage in practice. The schools should make presentation techniques an important part of the program and ensure that all serious juries include a highly vocal and thoroughly versatile, if not quarrelsome, nonarchitect. Similarly, the written word should be given more attention. Letters, proposals, feasibility studies, and planning reports are part and parcel of today's practice. The time spent putting these together and the low level of competence reflected can often cloud an otherwise good client relationship. If projects are stalled and the building is never built, the planning report is the "finished product." It is important that it be well done.

verbal communication and presentation essential ingredients of the architect's training

No formal education can ever prepare a man for all the complexities, subtle interrelationships, or practical problems that face him in the world of work. But a much more serious effort could be made by architectural schools to prepare the student for the exigencies of practice. Only experience can teach the psychology of a truly responsive client or business relationship, but the student can learn in school something of the context in which he will have to work. It should not come as a shock to him that design ability—God-given talent though it is—can be a very frail flower against the cold wind of reality.

To prepare for this, architectural curricula must obviously be broadened in scope. Interdisciplinary and multidisciplinary training must be conducted at a number of different levels, and the architect must begin to specialize in school. Because architecture is practiced by a team composed of designers, planners, and landscape, structural, mechanical, and electrical engineers who will sometimes need the services of experts in acoustics, aerodynamics, and agronomy—to mention only a few—it seems logical that these specialists be exposed to one another at an early stage of their educations. And since architects have to deal with clients—lawyers, scientists, politicians, and real estate and business executives—this multidisciplinary relationship should start at school and become part of professional training.

multidisciplinary training the foundation of the building team

Early specialization would solve the confusion that still arises in architectural schools through an undue emphasis on the talents of the designer. Only about 2 percent of the enrollment of the typical architectural school is really talented in creative conceptual design. But most students will have enrolled because of an interest in "design." During their education they become frustrated, because design is the all-consuming thrust, and there is no obvious place for them if their lack of creative design talent is too readily acknowledged. Yet the team practice of architecture has a desperate need for diverse talent in the related disciplines just discussed. It is often not until long after graduation that the student who is not a 'designer' finds his place in the team. We must try at school to rediscover the tree and its branches. Although I do not propose that students concentrating in engineering, construction management, or other closely related fields be excused from design—any more than I would excuse design majors from engineering—the emphasis in these courses should be different. Each student, through this changed emphasis, would become aware of his own and others' roles in the complex process of making buildings. The curriculum should be so structured that it allows for integration—over the drawing board—of the teaching of technical and professional subjects with that of conceptual design.

shades of emphasis in the architectural curriculum

The artificial divisions between design, building science, economics, social science, and related fields, which have made true teamwork so difficult, should be broken down in school. The graduate should emerge with some competence in all the fields that form the base of his professional career and with an understanding of the roles these disciplines will play in the design process. But he should specialize in his special aptitude as soon as he realizes where it lies.

The too prevalent method of architectural education, which leaves many of the decisions on course material and problem types to the individual instructor, is too chancy in a world of rigorous demands and complex pressures. Students who cannot count on a continuous and progressive educational experience are led into the taboos and mystical attitudes that have dogged the profession and blunted its effectiveness. Much of the time we are brilliantly solving the wrong problems.

A master syllabus based on the case system should be developed. For instance, those architects concentrating on planning could do the basic research involved in setting the stage for design of a new city, for urban renewal, or for determining the growth pattern of an existing city. From this base, realistic case studies of every conceivable architectural problem could be devised—from the simplest piece of street furniture to buildings, to groups of buildings, to the texture of the city itself. Problems—progressing from the most basic to the most complex—should be presented so that the student becomes acquainted in an orderly fashion with the entire spectrum of architectural experience.

As the curriculum progresses to the more advanced and complex problems, students from other disciplines— sociology, law, government, economics, finance—should become part of the course structure, for the problems of the city and urban living form the base of their case studies also. The architectural student would learn how projects are financed and promoted, and the other students would gain an insight into design goals and processes. This is the knowledge that prepares the student for the real world, in which the man who controls housing is not the man who lives in it but the man who invests his money in it.

the case study approach educates architects and clients together

Why shouldn't it augur well for the future if all these disciplines learn, in depth, at an early age, to work together, understand the strengths and problems of each other's profession, and break down the barriers of negative attitude and misunderstanding that have so seriously hindered communication? We would be educating architects and clients at the same time. I would hazard a guess that at present architects spend 30 to 40 percent of their on-the-job time in educating their clients. And clients probably feel the same way. The time could be used more productively in getting on with the job, in pursuing a common goal.

All of this means that architecture, as it is presently defined, along with several closely related disciplines, must become the one profession of environmental design.

The profession of architecture is, of course, already completely within this framework, and some schools are placed within this context. Branches of engineering are now functioning within this framework, but vast areas of related human endeavor remain outside it. The profession yet to be brought to full flower is one wherein the potent gravitational force of the new practice will draw a wider range of professionals into a closer—and thus much more effective—unity.

an educated public essential to the future of architecture

It is evident that the planning and building of our cities require more than the wisdom and practical experience of experts in many fields. They also need the intuitive feeling of the artist and—above all—the lively and learning interest of the human beings who will live in them. The greatest challenge for educated men and women today is to heighten their awareness of the potential quality of life and of the ways in which design can lift burdens and extend horizons and create a climate in which good living is possible. The design professions, however well trained, can do little in unfertile soil. The purpose of architecture, as defined by my late colleague Eero Saarinen, is everyone's purpose: "Man is on earth for a very short time, and he is not quite sure what his purpose is. Religion gives him his primary purpose. The permanence and beauty and meaningfulness of his surroundings give him confidence and a sense of continuity. So to the question, what is the purpose of architecture? I would answer—to shelter and enhance man's life on earth and to fulfill his belief in the nobility of his existence."

the quality of the environment is a matter of choice

Today, architecture is no longer an articulation of tradition or a search for a new style. A new style is not created by every generation, although each succeeding generation assumes its duty is to do so. In truth, architecture must be an approach toward life—a life no longer simple—and it cannot help but reflect the profound disturbance of our age. The fact that we know how to build a 100-story building or an astrodome ballpark doesn't imply indiscriminate use of this technology. The great question for American architecture in the next decade is whether society will continue to demand incessant innovation for its own sake or will begin to select the ideas most worthy of development and perfection—will in fact make a choice in favor of humanity.

MEANING

To the question "What is architecture?" there are at once many answers and no answer. We are approaching the crux of the matter, and yet we are dealing with something we can neither easily analyze nor define. Should we even try to define a concept so subjective and so elusive? Or should we take the advice of the philosopher Wittgenstein, "whereof one cannot speak, thereof one must be silent"?

In trying to answer this question we are most poetic. "Suddenly you touch my heart," said Le Corbusier, "and I say this is beautiful, this is architecture." "A great building," said Louis Kahn, "must in my opinion begin with the unmeasurable and go through the measurable in the process of design, but must again in the end be unmeasurable." And for Breuer, "this question concerns the demand that the building, the street, the square, the city and the road over the land . . . speak of a mental surplus, or an emotional plus, of a conceptual generosity; of a stance which is optimistic and creative as a growing child's attention."

definitions, poetic and philosophical, share belief in architecture's value to man's spiritual and physical well-being

It is difficult for the architect to know if the people living and working in his buildings will experience them as he conceived them. What is it that, when all the program requirements are satisfied, makes one building beautiful and another simply not? How do we know that what we find beautiful now won't appear trite or even ugly to future generations? Think of the Victorian buildings—gross monstrosities to our grandparents— some of which we are now struggling to preserve.

Think of the Parthenon, which has appeared beautiful to every generation since it was built. Do we care, or should we care what future generations think of our buildings? Can we project what they will think? Can we even be sure that buildings built today will survive that long? If we pursue beauty, are we pursuing vanity? Are we forgetting our clients' needs and lapsing into glorification of ourselves?

but how do we approach spiritual well-being? Beauty and delight are difficult to project

Hard and paradoxical questions; but the way they have been answered through the generations is the key to architectural criticism and the fads and fashions of architecture.

Monumentality and virtuosity are out of style today, perhaps in response to a definite and regrettable trend toward virtuosity at the expense of program requirements, but it is too easy to brand attempts at perfection—attempts that fail— as unfulfilled ego trips.

The current emphasis on flexibility and accelerated construction may have led us to justify mediocrity and anonymity too easily. A building cannot be all things to all men at all times.

superficial concern with trends has weakened architectural criticism

Competition and communication through our journals have an impact on our approach, but in following fashion and in failing to analyze the enduring qualities of a building, architectural criticism in this country has (in my opinion) done a disservice to our profession and to the public. The demand by the architectural press for conformity to the mode of the moment has almost encouraged the proliferation of cyclical, stylized cliches.

Architects should not design for their critics or for the award programs, although, admittedly, the temptation is hard to resist.

Of course, architectural criticism is needed, but to be useful it must be conducted in a more serious spirit, not just to "publish to survive" or to promote newsworthy controversy.

Program difficulties and budget limitations are never an excuse for a bad building, although they sometimes make great architecture impossible. An analysis of the process and context of architecture and its effect on design would be valid criticism and an education to architect and client alike. It is not necessary for all architecture to be "great"—this should be understood. Most of it is "background" or environmental architecture, but it is no less important and should be taken seriously.

Buildings are built, after all, to fulfill specific needs and to adapt to existing environments. Their ability to do this should form part of any critical study, whether or not they meet the less easily defined aesthetic and cultural standards of a current design vocabulary. Architectural critics would do the profession and public a profound service if they could help us draw the line between egotistic dreams and reality.

there is some common basis for projection and evaluation of building solutions

Despite the idiosyncrasies in taste and the vagaries of style, which vary with individuals and generations, we are not, after all, designing in a void. We can rely on some basic common response to proportion, heat, ventilation, light, color, space, sound, texture, light and shadow in projecting a building concept. Indeed, the psychophysics of human response to some of these elements has been quite well researched and documented. But what cannot be so readily documented is the overlaid emotional content of people's experience—their memories, their associations, the social or economic strata associated with different kinds of building materials, the prestige or vanity factor and the fads and fashions of the times. And perhaps above all, it is difficult for people to detach themselves from a known environment and allow themselves to respond in an unprejudiced way to something new. When a building is right, it is almost universally sensed and accepted, although people may not know why.

Whereas there is obviously no blueprint for architecture—as I have tried to define it—I have developed over the years some guidelines within which a building should at least be good and has the potential, if appropriate, to be great.

I have a deep respect for function. The planning problems must be solved. The building must not only work for the user but also, if possible, be flexible for the future. Structure is of great importance. It should be forthright, logical, honest. It should have integrity, which does not mean that structure should necessarily be expressed. A building should express in some way its purpose as well as have unity in itself. It must be a whole thing, rather than a lot of pieces strung together. Integration within the environment is important, for, if we are to avoid the physical chaos with which we are now surrounded, we must respect to some extent the existing fabric, be it natural or man-made. In the long view, to be new and exciting may not be as important as to be courteous and restrained. But this does not mean that—within these parameters—we should not exploit fully the technology and materials we have at our command.

some general guidelines for design integrity

Perhaps most of all it is important to realize that at any time we are only a link between the past and the future, and we must see ourselves as evolving from the one and leading to the other—despite the ever-present temptation to deny our forebears. Since in the last analysis architecture reflects society's priorities and purposes, our architectural heritage is a unique expression of the history and progress of man. What monuments we leave behind in the form of buildings reveal more clearly than anything else the value we place on the quality of life.

Conceptual design—when materials should come together into visual form—is the part of the architectural process or experience most difficult to analyze. Sometimes the basic idea for a building seems to "come in a flash" and—like Archimedes—the architect, figuratively at least, jumps out of the bath or shower and shouts "Eureka!" But, even if this experience occurs within an individual mind, it is really much more of a group endeavor than we designers are often willing to admit.

the evolution of the building concept

The first meetings with clients, the discussions, the program, the alternative solutions mulled over in the office that have been "cooking in the subconscious mind" all contribute to the conceptualization. In certain instances, however, this flash of inspiration does not seem to occur. Sometimes one has to "slog through" the problem detail by detail and stage by stage, and it is only after an arduous process of evaluation and reevaluation that the idea for the building is born.

In cases like this, the idea, when it comes, is sometimes quite different from the direction all the slogging has seemed to take. So, quite late in the game, one appears to be scrapping all the work that has been done and starting again. What one has, in fact, done is work through and reject all the alternatives before reaching a conceptual conclusion.

The relation of time to problem solving is of great significance and worthy of mention, not to say further study. Why does it take so long to develop solutions when the concept has already been reached? In the fifteenth century Leonardo thought of the flying machine, yet man didn't take to the air until the Wright brothers' feat of 1907. Similarly, solar energy is a theoretical reality, but practical applications are still some years away. In my own practice, we developed an aluminum sandwich wall panel in the 1940s, but the product has only just been introduced to the market. The idea—and the theory— are not enough. Technology, industry, economics, and psychological acceptance have to be tuned to a fine balance before a concept becomes a solution. Perhaps the future of our environment—and even of our civilization—depends on our learning to speed up or telescope this process. For time is no longer on our side.

Of course, the finished building is never one man's work. Engineering and construction disciplines have a tremendous input into design, and that is why the possessive instinct linking the individual architect to his design is something of a delusion.

Now, having said all that, one cannot deny the creative or artistic impulse as an essential element of architecture. There is a little bit of the prima donna in all creative people, whether in arts, letters, business, or science. And of course you have to fall in love with your ideas or you wouldn't have the impetus or stamina to complete them.

In my experience in architectural practice, I find that people's subjective reactions to the process and product of architecture become part of the content of the subconscious mind. I am a great believer in the role of the subconscious in what we often—and perhaps mistakenly—classify as the intuitive approach to design. Whereas I have always thought of myself as an intuitive designer, as someone to whom the basic concept may occur before all the data and programming information have been assembled and weighed, some of the younger designers in my office seem to work less intuitively; they assemble the data and proceed from the detailed analysis of these to the concept. I have come to think that this difference is largely a function of age and experience. I am relying on the principles and data collected over the years from many projects and many clients, to perform more quickly and less self-consciously what, as a younger man, I did more painstakingly and with greater apparent documentation. Thus much of what we describe as intuition may in fact be a question of synthesis.

analysis of design synthesis rids the architectural process of some of its mystery

But, whatever the true nature of intuition, we must beware of relying on it as a mystical "leap" that allows us to bypass the steps along the way. If intuition has a strong empirical content, this must be documented to create a more tangible basis for design decisions and to allow objective discussion and evaluation instead of the after-the-fact rationalizations of whimsicality, in which, as a profession, we have become expert!

Sometimes what are conceived as intuitive solutions may in reality be an adaptation of some kind of universal theme, not necessarily best suited to the specific needs of the client.

Oddly enough, the architect, who has nursed his concept so carefully and possessively while it is still only a concept, tends to cut the umbilical cord completely once the building becomes part of the public experience. Does he ever really find out how people respond to and use his buildings? Unless the architect–client relationship is particularly close, or conversely, unless there are problems and complaints with which he had to deal, he all too often abandons his offspring once it is out in the world. Yet there is much to be learned in watching a building grow and change over a period of years in response to the needs and activities of its users—much that could be fed back into the design experience to become part of the objective language of architecture.

the completed building a valuable but neglected source of knowledge

15

Urban Architecture

Talking about the problems of cities—like talking about the problems of the human race—induces the same feelings of apathy or helplessness. But even if man's lot is philosophically unacceptable, most of us want to live as long as we can. Even though cities are basically impossible places, people will continue to want to live in them.

Our inability to change the human condition fundamentally does not mean that we cannot significantly affect the quality of individual lives. And our failure to grapple successfully with the total nightmare of megalopolis does not mean that we cannot solve some of the problems of specific cities and neighborhoods or that efforts to improve the quality of urban life are necessarily doomed before they are started.

In some respects at least the climate for significant urban design is better than it has been. One reason is that cities have been quite well researched, and exposure has been given to the resultant theories of urban planning. There have been studies of the aging of buildings, research into patterns of growth and change in cities, and well-documented reports on the new towns of Europe. Theories of the form, content, and dynamics of cities—as different as Jane Jacobs' and Soleri's—have reached the public consciousness through books, magazines, and museums. Although there is no consensus on solutions, there has been considerable analysis of the problems. The public has itself become involved in urban planning. Zoning regulations—their use and abuse—have penetrated community groups who have organized to fight or encourage zoning changes in their own neighborhoods. Advocacy planning and community involvement have become buzz words of the profession. And there are success stories (as well as failures) to add impetus to fresh efforts. Renewal of the waterfronts of San Francisco and Boston, the regeneration of Philadelphia, the blossoming of Atlanta—all encourage the belief that improvement is possible.

In New York and other cities, incentives to developers to include public amenities in their urban programs have made possible the mixed-use development employed in the design for the First National City Bank in New York. Whereas this creates tremendous opportunities, it is also a considerable challenge for the architect who finds himself working for a highly complex, not always constant or immediately recognized client group. The major client clearly dominates the overall direction of the project, but the ultimate solution has to satisfy the needs of a much wider public. It is important to define this wider group and ensure that the planning process is open to their input before basic decisions are frozen.

In New York, for example, the primary concern is to meet the corporate goals of the First National City Bank in a building whose functional, social, aesthetic, and symbolic values must converge. We are also working with a vitally involved community church whose social and religious endeavors demand both outreach and meditation. And then we are designing for the office workers who will work every day within the tower; for the general public who will miss the little stores and restaurants that used to cover the block—and who desperately need an opportunity to escape from the grid and find somewhere to sit in the shade and eat a sandwich; and for the future generations of tenants who may want to adapt the buildings for very different uses. All these are in an important sense clients—clients whose needs are not in every respect the same and may sometimes be frankly contradictory.

A complication of the corporate structure that may affect the smoothness of a building program is the frequent and often sudden change of the executive hierarchy. To maintain continuity and momentum through this disruption requires positive effort by both architect and client. The architect must be aware of the importance of documenting every step in the programming and design development so that he can explain and support his decisions to a new client representative. However constructive personal rapport may be in the creative process, it cannot be relied upon to carry a job through to a successful conclusion. Similarly, the client must be prepared to brief incoming staff on the background and progress of decision making. If he does not make provision for continuity in spite of personnel change, he is risking considerable loss of time and possible "watering down" of the basic design concept. The early stages of a major urban job are really an educational process, and perhaps if they were recognized as such, some of the difficulties would not occur or would at least be minimized. The team, and this includes the client, have to get used to one another. For this reason, if for no other, it is desirable that the full team be assembled as early as possible in the planning process.

1 view from the south
2 midtown silhouette

1

Citicorp Center, New York, 1972

The opportunity to plan and design the buildings for an entire city block is a rare and exciting challenge for any architectural firm—particularly when the city is New York, and the block, between Lexington and Third Avenues, 53rd and 54th Streets—is in the heart of midtown Manhattan.

Citicorp Center is much more than a conventional office tower. It is a unique condominium development combining on one site a major urban church; a low-rise building containing executive offices, retail stores, boutiques, and restaurants that overlook a skylit atrium; a 65-story office tower; a landscaped plaza with subway access; and a through-block arcade. The challenge to the architects was to meet the individual needs, corporate and financial goals, and civic obligations of a complex client group within a unified scheme that would enrich the texture of the urban environment and add a more vital yet relaxed dimension to crowded midtown life.

In the hands of the First National City Bank, a corporate client with a strong sense of public responsibility, the new development will bring to New Yorkers the imaginative urban experience that is so vital and important but that has, until recently, been obliterated by corporate development in midtown.

At 914 feet the tower is the third highest in midtown Manhattan and the fifth highest in New York City. The angled roof plane—with its potential for solar energy collection—expresses the technology of our time. In so doing, a new concept emerges identifying Citicorp within the New York skyscraper hierarchy. It also relieves the uniformity of flat-topped towers proliferating in the center of the city. New York's first tall buildings were notable for the elaborate, romantic, and sometimes witty domes and spires that made them unique. The survivors from this era provide New York's skyline with its world-renowned identity.

To accommodate this diversity of function and the large enclosed areas within the limits of the city block, the office

2

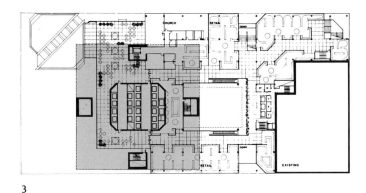

3

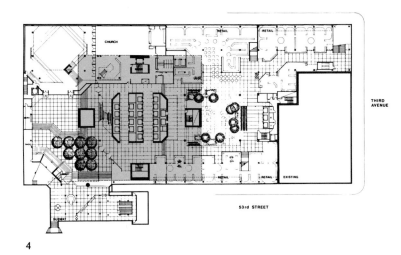

4

3 second-level plan
4 concourse plan
5 street-level plan
6 typical tower floor plan
7 view from plaza

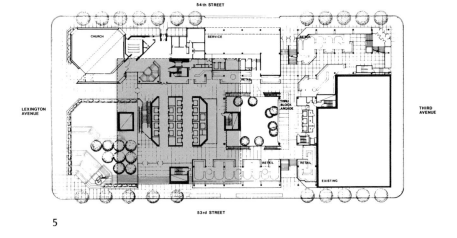

5

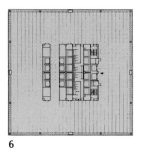

6

tower has been lifted on 115-foot-high supercolumns placed at midsection instead of—more conventionally—at the corners of the building. This brings light and air to the pedestrian areas and enables the church and the low-rise-building to be grouped or "nestled" around the base of the office tower without being crowded. The four office floors overlooking the atrium step back beneath the tower to gain extra light and potential terrace space. The 9000-square-foot pedestrian plaza is depressed below street level to give it easy access from the subway, provide some seclusion from the noise and bustle of the street, and relate it to the main sanctuary space of St. Peter's Church, also on this same level.

The glass-enclosed tower lobby is approached at street level from both Lexington Avenue and 53rd Street. This lobby and "through-block arcade" converge onto the shop-lined, skylit atrium. The tower thus becomes the focus of a vital and varied stream of urban life.

20

7

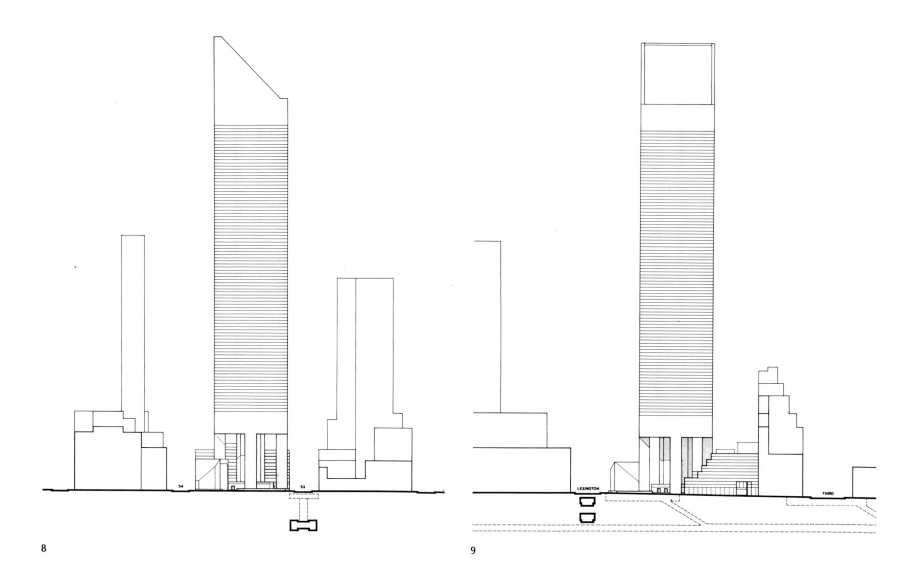

8 west elevation
9 south elevation
10 skylit atrium

8

9

10

The square office tower is planned around a central elevator and service core to give maximum flexibility to the office floors. Doubledeck elevators—an innovation in this building—allow simultaneous loading at concourse and street levels, channeling circulation and at the same time reducing the space and power required for conventional elevator equipment.

Sheathed in alternate bands of reflective glass and gleaming aluminum, the tower makes a powerful thrust into the era of space-age architecture. Trees, shrubs, flowers, pools, bright-colored awnings, and street furniture add warmth, vitality, and human scale to the pedestrian areas.

The building's steel structure employs a system of diagonal chevron bracing in the exterior surfaces to transfer wind and gravity loads through the columns to the foundations. The system allows maximum column-free space within the building, and—since the diagonal chevrons are exposed *within* rather than outside the bands of glass—an opportunity exists for dynamic interior treatment.

The wind problem associated with lightly framed tall buildings is considerable, and, because of this, wind tunnel tests are becoming a necessary procedure. As a result of these tests, Citicorp Center may have in its penthouse the United States' first tuned mass damper, to dampen excessive movement inherent in a tall building.

From its inception Citicorp Center has been designed with energy conservation as a prime program requirement. The square tower and atrium plan for the low-rise building produces a high ratio of interior space to exterior area. Only

46 percent of the exterior surface is glass, for which a reflective double-paned glass is to be used. Baffled low-brightness light fixtures reduce the wattage needed to provide acceptable light levels, which are varied according to intensity of use. Zone control of the tower permits air conditioning to be supplied to specific floors while others are shut off when not needed. The system, which makes maximum use of outside air in good weather conditions, is equipped with special filters to clean recycled air and reduce fresh air intake when conditioning is needed. A tunnel connection with the bank's existing offices at 399 Park Avenue will permit operation of both buildings from a single power plant during offpeak times.

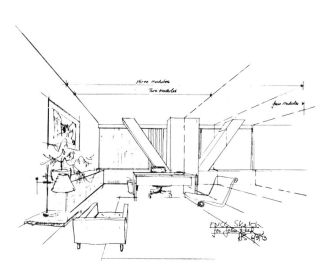

11

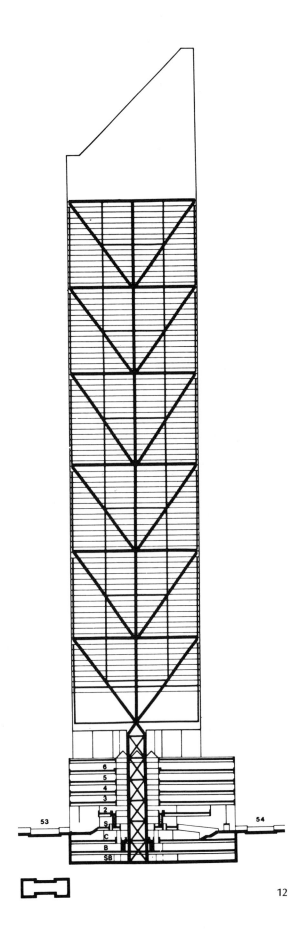

11   office with chevron bracing
12   chevron bracing in exterior wall system

12

25

13 perspective, original concept
14 model, original concept

The building's management system will be based on computer operation that will automatically match the flow of energy to actual demand. Energy can be stored in the building to reduce reliance on purchased energy in peak periods.

On a project of this kind, feasibility and design studies have to begin before site acquisition is completed and, indeed, before it is certain how much of the site will ultimately be acquired. This accentuates the architect's role, in that he will almost certainly have to prepare a number of alternatives. The Citicorp site took 5 years to acquire. During this period of site acquisition, seven alternative studies were prepared for four possible sites, and the scheme finally accepted has itself been through radical and detailed design development.

The modified bonus system, which allows developers extra rentable floor area in exchange for the inclusion of public facilities in the overall plan, has enabled the Citicorp project to make a considerable contribution to the urban environment of New York. When the first design study was developed, it appeared that zoning changes would make it possible to include luxury housing units in the penthouse of the tower. This was one reason for the angled top of the structure, to allow stepped balconies for each south-facing apartment. This zoning change did not materialize, and the housing was dropped from the scheme.

This initial concept placed the elevator and service elements in a detached core, which had the advantages of leaving the office floors open for tenants to plan as they wished and of providing a potential area of refuge from fire. A number of other functional advantages were also provided, as well as an exciting and beautiful form. But problems arose with the potential rentability of the office space, because conventional office floors with a central core seemed more popular on the New York rental market.

14

Unionmutual Offices, Portland, Maine, 1967

The long, low profile of this office building evolved in response to the client's requirement for open, flexible office floors and to the rolling character of the Maine countryside. As much as possible of the wooded site was preserved in its natural state and parking kept away from the long facade facing the Maine Turnpike. The two upper levels of the building are sheathed in mirror glass, so that views of the building from the highway are dramatized by reflections of earth, trees, and clouds mirrored in the facade. The lower level is slightly recessed to accent the floating "mirror-bar" in the landscape.

The 420 foot long bar containing about 215,000 square feet of flexible office space is planned for expansion to almost double this area to meet future needs. Long-span steel construction

1

minimizes interior columns to make it as easy as possible to adapt office layouts to changing work patterns. Individual and group insurance operations are located on the upper two floors, with executive and staff facilities and all support functions below.

An open court—rising from the first to the third level—gives focus and a change of scale to the expansive interior. Functioning as a reception area or exhibit space, the court can be thought of as a gateway to the building—a crossroads or transition space for the building's staff and visitors.

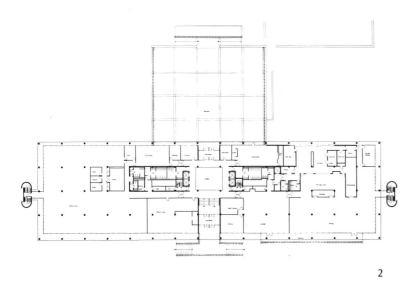

2

3

1 view from the south
2 groundfloor plan
3 typical floor plan
4 fire stair and reflective glass
5 entrance detail
6 elevation

4

5

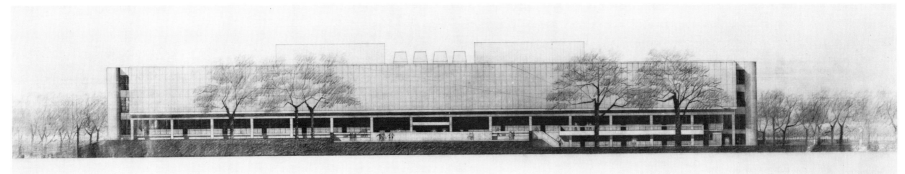

6

Back Bay Center Project, Boston, 1953

An imaginative collaborative scheme to transform a desolate railroad yard (now the site of the Prudential Center) to a mixed-use urban center was thought of as the "spearhead of the city's economic war against its suburbs." By providing extensive below-grade parking with a multilevel pedestrian circulation system above and by mixing high-rise and lower rise office buildings, stores, a balconied motor hotel, and a domed convention center around a series of landscaped walks and plazas, it was hoped to attract people back into the center of the city. The design team included Pietro Belluschi, The Architects Collaborative, Walter F. Bogner, Hugh Stubbins, and Carl Koch. Before the advent of the "team" as an official buzz word of the profession, this project was an example of a high-level collaborative effort. There was no slicing of the problem into parts; a separate Boston Center Architects office was set up, and it took only 3 months to produce the scheme.

Teachers College, Columbia University
New York, 1967

The master plan for expansion of this institution covers the entire block between Broadway and Amsterdam Avenue and 121st and 122nd Streets in New York.

The plan provides for several floors of below-grade parking. The street level contains commercial space for shops and concessions with entrances to a linear, three-story mall running east-west through the site. Around the mall are grouped classrooms, lecture halls, laboratories, faculty offices, and other academic facilities. The roof of this block is developed as a landscaped area—a garden in the sky—from which rise two residential towers for students and faculty. It is anticipated that some of the residential space will be occupied by people from the neighborhood displaced by the development.

The entire complex is connected to older campus buildings to the south via the central library, which spans 121st Street. The library in the geographic center becomes the heart of the institution.

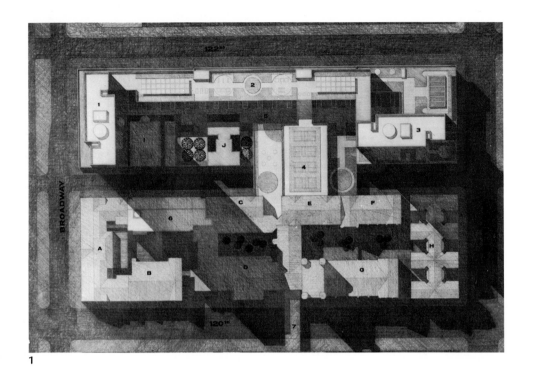

1

1 rendered site plan
2 longitudinal section
3 aerial view from the southeast

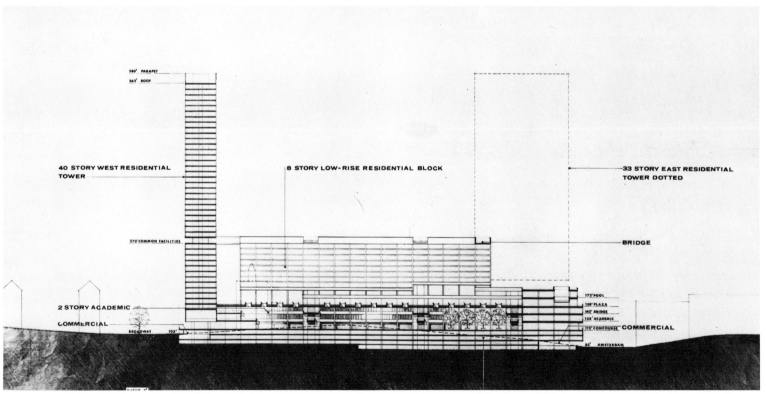

2

3

1

1 principal facade
2 Hugh Stubbins' office
3 reception area
4 work area

1033 Massachusetts Avenue, Cambridge, 1967

When the firm outgrew rented offices in Cambridge, we decided to develop our own new building. In association with consulting engineers LeMessurier Associates (structural engineers for this and many other of our buildings) and Dupree Associates, a parcel of land was developed at 1033 Massachusetts Avenue to provide home offices, some 84,000 square feet of rental office space, plus 6000 square feet for retail/commercial use.

The six-story facade of the building was designed with the scale of Cambridge in mind, to respect the existing street building line and maintain a strong but simple expression of the building's function. Concrete on both poured-in-place columns and precast spandrels is painted light brown to blend with the predominant tone of the buildings in the neighborhood. Windows are straightforward spans of glass between the concrete.

In the Hugh Stubbins and Associates offices on the sixth floor and part of the fifth, the space is essentially simple and open, associates' offices and cubicles flanking the open drafting room. Partitions between the drafting room and the windows are glass, giving everyone a view of the outside. This "see through" feature is carried throughout the offices, affording everyone outside light and delightful "treetop" views of the city and the neighboring Boston skyline. All furniture, including drafting tables and dividers, was designed by our team.

The street floor is set back beneath the projection of the upper floors to widen the pavement and—with the help of planting—give an arcade-like quality to the sidewalk. The building is identified at the main entry by a bold supergraphic rendition of Merle Westlake's *1033*.

2

3

4

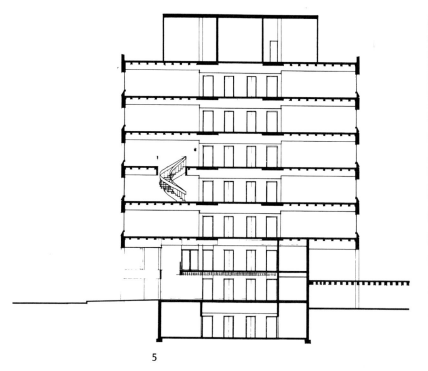

5

6

7

8

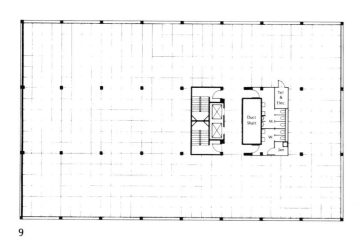

9

10

The typical office floor has some 12,000 square feet of space with the service core placed off center. LeMessurier's offices on the third and fourth floors are connected by a private staircase. Partitioning throughout the building follows a 2-foot module, and where partitions connect with a glass surface rather than a column, they are connected by simple neoprene gaskets to prevent any disruption of the exterior rhythm of the building.

Covered parking is accessible from Massachusetts Avenue or from the entry level inside the building; open parking at the rear of the building can be reached from a side street or from the mezzanine level.

Although Massachusetts Avenue is a prime artery through Cambridge, the quality of its development is patchy, petering out in this area to an anonymous mixture of service stations, cinemas, apartments, snackbars, and small shops. Developing new offices has helped provide a focus for upgrading this part of the avenue. Two other new office buildings have now been completed nearby, and high-quality furniture and clothing stores have moved into the commercial space.

5 cross section
6 principal elevation
7 office
8 sidewalk view
9 typical floor plan
10 entrance detail

1

Federal Reserve Bank of Boston, 1970

Three main forces converged to shape the design of this complex: the importance of a clear expression of distinct but related functions in a unified scheme that would enhance a prime renewal area of downtown Boston, the need for well-defined circulation, and the requirement for a high level of security within a pleasant environment.

To conduct its complex banking functions and provide stimulation and a sense of fulfillment for its employees, the Federal Reserve Bank required several different kinds of space. Maximum security areas were needed for coin, currency, and check operations. A major banking operation; light, attractive space for executive and administrative functions; rentable floors; and imaginative employee facilities were all essential parts of the program.

Careful study of program and organizational requirements led to the decision to place the secure areas, needing large floors, in a separate low-rise block and the office floors in a high-rise tower giving employees the advantages of daylight and views over the city and the harbor. To integrate the two elements within a single, unified scheme, a connecting link was designed to house employee facilities, public gallery/display area, and the central security control station—strategically located with a view over the whole complex. By placing the employee floor and recreation facilities at the top of the low-rise building, it was possible to make them accessible to everyone working in the complex and to provide the added amenity of a landscaped roof garden.

Since the secure areas are to some extent inward looking—while the office areas are perceived as open, receptive, outgoing—the low-rise building forms a U-shaped configuration around and connected to the tower. A landscaped court with pools emphasizes the humanity of the buildings in an urban setting and creates an effective transition between them.

The opening beneath the office floors expresses the change in function between public and office space while making visible the link between the office tower and the rest of the complex. It also lightens the effect of the tower so that it appears to stand freely above the rest of the complex.

This opening is also a helpful element in reducing the downward force of the wind around the building base. By allowing the air to escape from the high- to low-pressure zone via the opening, it diverts the wind's force from the pedestrian entrances and walkways below.

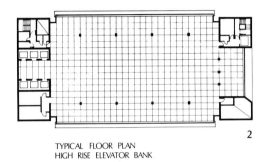

TYPICAL FLOOR PLAN
HIGH RISE ELEVATOR BANK

2

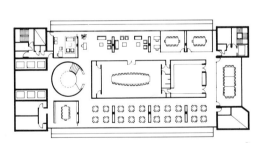

BOARD ROOM / EXECUTIVE DINING LEVEL
31st FLOOR

3

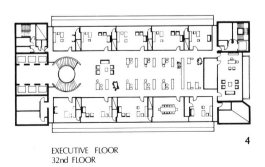

EXECUTIVE FLOOR
32nd FLOOR

4

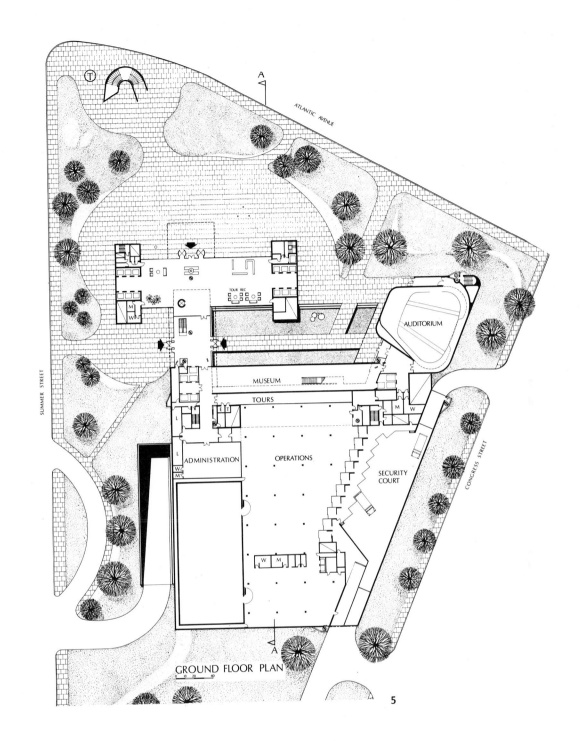

GROUND FLOOR PLAN

5

1   model from the east
2   typical floor plan
3   executive dining and boardroom floor
4   executive offices
5   groundfloor and site plan

6

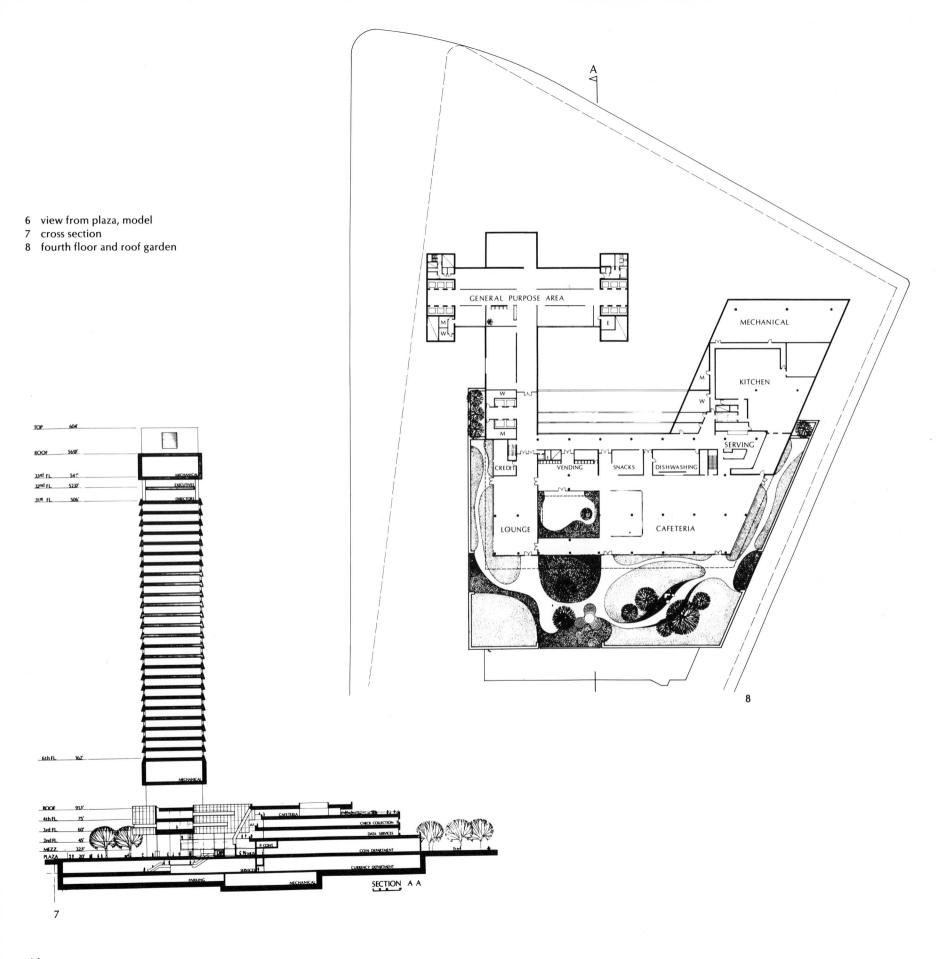

6 view from plaza, model
7 cross section
8 fourth floor and roof garden

GENERAL PURPOSE AREA

MECHANICAL

KITCHEN

SERVING

CREDIT   VENDING   SNACKS   DISHWASHING

LOUNGE   CAFETERIA

8

TOP   604'
ROOF   568'
33rd FL   541'   MECHANICAL
32nd FL   523'   EXECUTIVES
31st FL   506'   DIRECTORS

6th FL   162'   MECHANICAL

ROOF   91.5'   CAFETERIA
4th FL   75'   CHECK COLLECTION
3rd FL   60'   DATA SERVICES
2nd FL   45'
MEZZ   32.5'   P. CONT.   COIN DEPARTMENT
PLAZA   20'   SERVICES   CURRENCY DEPARTMENT
                  PARKING   MECHANICAL   SECTION A A

7

9

Open, flexible office floors that would lend themselves to an office landscape interior treatment were part of the program. Service cores are thus located at each end of the tower instead of in the middle, leaving large, clear spans of virtually column-free space in between. By holding the few columns away from the exterior walls, we were able to give uninterrupted glass windows to the office floors. Outside and above the glass, projecting aluminum spandrels ("eyebrows")—triangular in section—which produce the textured effect in the building form, serve as sunshades to shield the windows from solar heat gain in the summer while allowing the sun to reach the glass in winter. They also help to solve the wind problem associated with tall buildings by "spoiling" the downward acceleration of air, which causes discomfort around the base of tall buildings.

An exceptional site next to the South Station development in

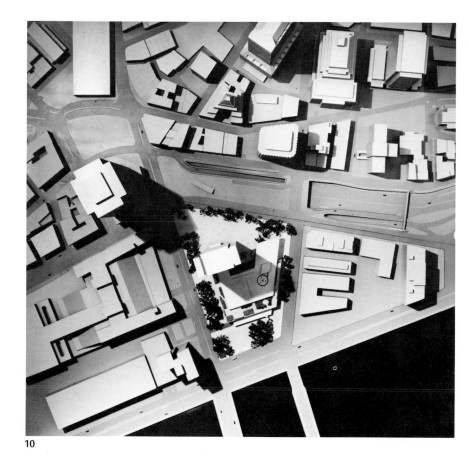

10

Boston's financial core permitted us to provide for future expansion and to include extensive landscaping unusual in a dense urban situation. Grassy banks, trees, and walkways surround the building. Pools provide a kind of "water court" between the tower and the low-rise structure. The employee facilities—which include cafeteria, store, kitchen, and roof terrace with views over Fort Point Channel—all recognize the importance to office workers of a relationship with the cityscape.

The client's commitment to a distinguished building, with people-oriented public spaces, and the brilliantly conceived engineering solution by LeMessurier Associates created a context in which architectural excellence was possible. If the Federal Reserve Bank is a successful building, it is the result of a sympathetic and enlightened client and the teamwork often talked about but not so often achieved.

11

1 hotel, office buildings, and covered plaza
2 concept plan and
3 sectional sketch by Hugh Stubbins

1

Spring Venture, Atlanta, 1974

A dramatic 9-acre site adjacent to Interstate Highway Route 75 promoted the concept of this development as the "northern gateway" to the burgeoning city of Atlanta. Two office towers, a luxury hotel, and an expansive, glass-enclosed, all-weather "pavilion" will sit atop a low-rise base structure covering almost the whole site. Spanning the north-south pairings of Spring Street (which gives the development its name), this base structure will contain some 600,000 square feet of leasable commercial–retail space. A 3500-seat auditorium and below-grade parking are included in the plan for the site, which also calls for the closing of several city streets and the provision of green space to soften and enhance the pedestrian character of the complex.

Integration of the different elements within a harmonious scheme is achieved by the unifying base structure, by the focus on the pavilion, and by the angled southern facade of the hotel, which protects the sloping glass enclosure from the afternoon sun and provides a defining edge or buttress to the new construction. With its strongly articulated, terraced structure, the 1200-room, 22-story hotel is designed to provide some exciting experiences of space, good views, and a readily identifiable physical form or orientation point—important in a convention city that is always full of visitors.

The slender, faceted profiles of the 75-story and 50-story office towers seem to belie the fact that they will be adding as much as 2.7 million square feet of office space to Atlanta's central business district. Sheathed in alternating bands of polished aluminum and double-paned reflective glass, the office towers are intended to create a light, buoyant feeling while at the same time making a contribution to energy conservation by controlling solar heat gain.

Within the climate-controlled 2-acre glass pavilion, a variety of activities will take place on many levels, including restaurants, boutiques, a film and entertainment center, and showrooms, and some of the hotel's function rooms will "hang" or cantilever out into the space.

A glass-enclosed, raised pedestrian walkway will link Spring Venture with the nearby rapid transit system and the developing residential and commercial complex on West Peachtree Street. The multimedia auditorium—planned as a separate structure south of Alexander Street—will add a significant entertainment facility to Atlanta's expanding cultural resources.

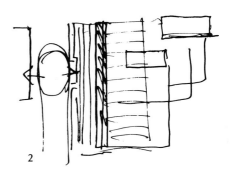

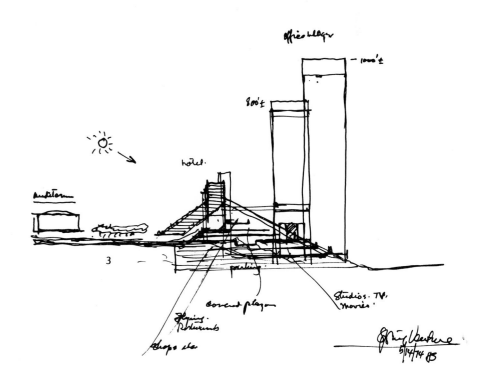

4

6

2

State Street Bank, Boston, 1964

A joint venture with Frederick A. Stahl and William J. LeMessurier, the design for this office tower was derived from an effort to break away from stereotyped office design and move toward a more efficient relation and ratio of circulation to office space.

Completed in 1965—primarily as a new home office for the State Street Bank and Trust Company, the 34-story tower has a ground-level public entrance and main banking hall, three 50,000-square-foot floors devoted to trust and executive functions of the bank, a fifth floor (with roof terrace) for personnel and executive/social functions, and 27 "typical" floors for bank or rental use. Two levels of parking and mechanical space are below grade. The third basement level is for safe deposit and bank vaults.

The plan, with its offset corners and deep cantilevers, provides for four additional corner offices per floor. Columns are expressed through the base structure to the street to minimize the impression of a tower supported on a podium.

The structure is steel frame with 17-foot cantilevered exterior spans—yielding a 15-foot depth for perimeter offices. Exterior walls are of precast concrete frame elements supported at each floor and glazed directly from the inside. There is, thus, no metal exposed to weather.

The lower floors of the building are compatible with the heights and a certain rustication of the surrounding nineteenth-century architecture, and the tower, with its very precise pattern of precast units, expresses the impact of modern technology on the urban scene.

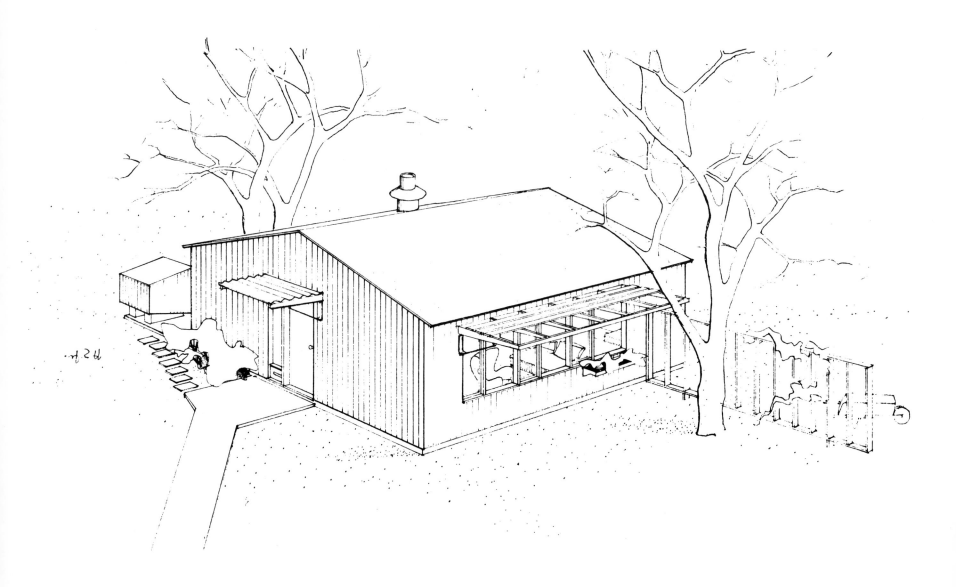

Houses

Despite regular predictions of its imminent demise—or survival only as an anachronism—the private house has remained at the core of the American dream of the good life. Shelter magazines sell more copies than ever, and there is probably no building type closer to the architect's heart.

When I started in practice, it was impossible for younger and smaller firms to get significant jobs. We were still at the tail end of the Depression, and there was not a lot of work around. In 1939, the war began to produce a demand for defense industry housing. Many architectural offices at that time were small, and most were involved in some form of house design. The house is good preparation for architectural practice—a good education. Designing a private house gives one—in a condensed form—experience of every activity in the making of a building. One is working with a client on something he cares deeply and personally about, and in a small office, one has to do everything himself—working drawings, mechanical layouts, construction supervision, and authorization of payments. We still find that the young architects who join our firm with this experience move more easily into larger scale work than those without it.

Houses have frequently been thought of as the architect's design research laboratory, but this approach should be adopted only with caution, lest the client's needs and desires get lost in the search for a new form. I remember once designing a house for a client who wanted a mantlepiece over the fireplace. I was completely enamored of the purity of my design concept and horrified that a mantlepiece would bastardize this chaste aesthetic. I won the battle, and the mantlepiece was omitted. Later I realized that, of course, she should have had a mantlepiece. I should have been able to bend my mind to designing one that would harmonize with the basic concept for the house.

House design is certainly an excellent education in communication, for in the close relationship that grows between client and architect, each begins to learn a good deal about the thought processes of the other. The expressed and unexpressed needs, the difficulty of projecting visual concepts or the experience of space, the way in which people really want to live—all these are an essential part of the language of architecture. In failing to understand how people use and react to their home territory, our profession has made some of its most serious mistakes, resulting on one occasion in pristine, new high-rise housing—unloved and finally abandoned by the people it was designed for.

So although a house sometimes affords opportunities for experiment with new spatial forms, expressing changes in life-style—Kiesler's endless house, perhaps, or Philip Johnson's glass pavilion—we cannot impose these ideas at the expense of the comfort and security of the people dwelling within them, unless we design houses for ourselves.

When I started into practice, I was fortunate. The American house was going through a kind of evolution. Glass walls, open planning, and exposed structural materials all reflected new construction techniques and an increasingly informal life-style that has remained with us. Some of my early houses thus still seem, I think, quite contemporary today.

1 original drawing by Hugh Stubbins
2 view from garden
3 plan
4 entrance side
5 living room
6 dining room
7 sheltered entrance

2

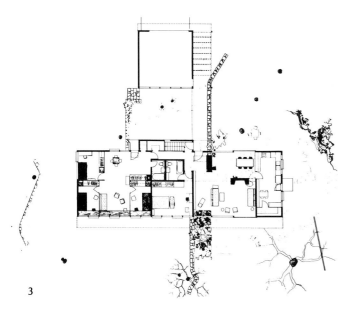

3

Stubbins' House (Lexington), 1946

My house in Lexington evolved from the family's need for expansive indoor–outdoor space for living and entertaining, with a flexible area for the three children, and a separate space for the office and studio with its own entry from the outside. Of course the site and personal attitudes influenced the concept in no small degree. The rectangular plan, its covered walk leading from the garage to a central entry to the house and its lower level studio tucked into the slope of the site, responds to all these needs. The children's bedrooms open off a shared work/play space, movable partitions allowing for a change in the arrangement as time passed. The bathrooms act as a buffer between the master bedroom and the entry area. Glass walls, terraces, an indoor garden—all reinforce the unity of the house with its site and reflect an increasing preoccupation with informal indoor–outdoor life-styles.

That the house was expanded twice proves the validity of its flexible plan.

4

5

6-7

Ryder House, 1949

The traditional New England "barn" house, with eave line raised to give usable loft space, inspired a contemporary expression of this building form in a summer house on Buzzard's Bay. By raising the eaves plate 3 feet 8 inches above the second floor line and opening the gable ends, I made the upper level fully usable at minimal extra cost. There is sufficent headroom for beds to be placed beneath the eaves along the outside walls. Since the house sits on wooded land sloping down to a beach, one wall is opened in glass to an expansive platform deck, which extends living space out toward the water. The opposite side opens into a walled-in patio—a sunny place to sit when the ocean breeze is too strong. Although designed as a summer cottage, the house was planned for eventual year-round use. Exposed structural beams and columns are stained dark to contrast with the silver gray siding and reinforce the building's relationship with barns in the area. Sunshades at the gable ends throw dramatic shadows on the end walls.

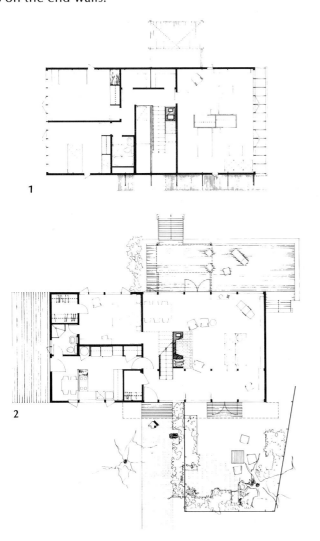

1

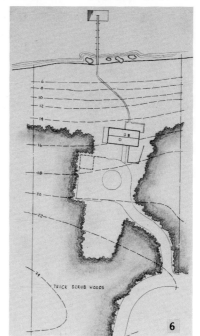

2

1 second-floor plan
2 first-floor plan
3 view from waterside
4 entrance
5 gable end
6 site plan

6

55

1

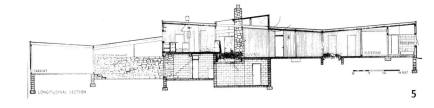

5

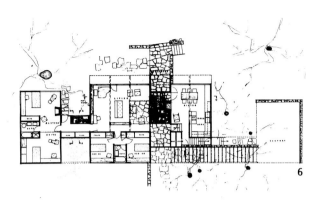

6

2

3

1 overall view
2,3 two fireplaces and garden
4 entrance
5 section
6 plan

4

Smith House, 1947

A light, airy house fitting naturally into the gently rolling site exploits the glass wall to take advantage of lovely views over the Connecticut River. The rectangular plan is essentially open—the double fireplace opposite the entrance screening the dining area and kitchen from the living room. Between the fireplaces an indoor garden flourishes beneath a sloping skylight, which also heightens the texture of the stone chimney. The angled roof planes reflect the contours of the site and open the house further to the sky and the view. The exposed modular framing system gives order and rhythm to the interior space. Natural white cedar walls, fir columns and beams, slate floors, and native stone retaining walls express the regional character in contemporary terms.

1

McCune House, 1947

On a wooded slope in the countryside near Boston, this house was designed for a growing family and planned for future expansion. A rocky outcropping on the site puts the entry, dining area, and kitchen on a slightly higher level than the living room. A skylit indoor garden emphasizes the separation of the living room from the entry and dining area while maintaining a continuous flow of space between them.

The structure consists of walls of 8 inch concrete block painted on both interior and exterior, stone-surfaced concrete floors, and a sloping wooden roof. By placing the entrance in the center of the plan and introducing two sheltered courtyards, effective zoning separation is achieved between the bedroom wing and the rest of the house. The living room is further extended with a cantilevered balcony giving access to the ground below.

3

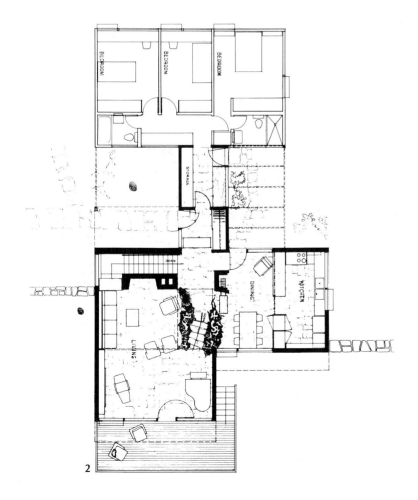

2

1 concept drawing by Hugh Stubbins
2 plan
3 dining area

59

1

2

Kronenberg House, 1948

Planned on a modular, post-and-beam construction system, this flat-roofed, single-story house contains three bedrooms, a study, maid's room, kitchen, and large, open living–dining area. The main entry leads into a paved gallery—flanked by the study and a small landscaped courtyard—at the end of which is the expansive living–dining space. The essentially H-shaped plan allows good separation of activities into three main zones: bedrooms—grouped together—living spaces, and service and utilities. The maid's room, kitchen, and laundry function as a buffer zone separating the service approach and garage from the main entry. The wood structural system is clearly expressed in both the interior and the exterior, which is sheathed with redwood siding. The site—a flat-topped, wooded knoll—yields fine views in several directions.

1 entrance side
2 plan
3 court
4 exterior detail
5 east elevation

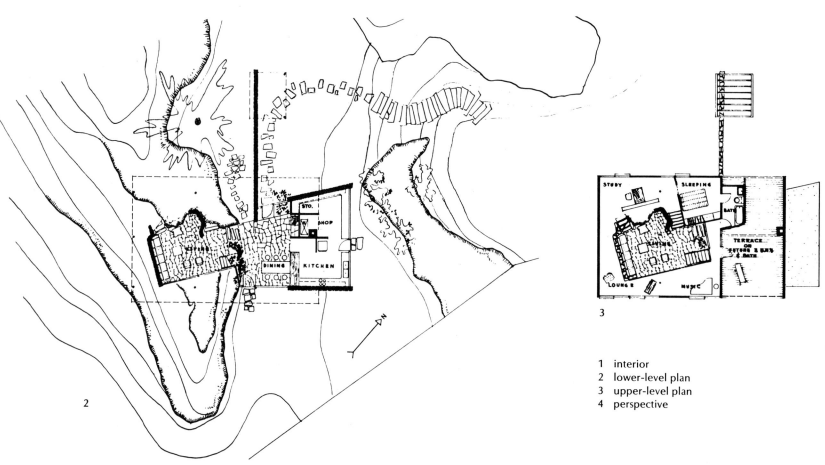

1 interior
2 lower-level plan
3 upper-level plan
4 perspective

Cockpit House, 1946

Perched above a rocky shoreline, this little house, designed for a bachelor, introduces an early version of the "conversation pit" surrounded by loosely defined areas for music, eating, relaxing, and sleeping. Kitchen and dining—plus expanded living space—are on a lower level, but open stairs through a rocky garden allow them to share the spatial volume of the house. The terrace is planned as a sun deck and for possible conversion to future bedroom use. The stone fireplace and the sunken sitting area give a sense of warmth and enclosure in a glass-walled, outward-looking beach retreat.

1

Keith House, 1950

The split level, now so commonplace even on flat sites, at this time was an innovative way of dealing with a sloping terrain while maintaining the open living spaces then becoming so popular. The site—a wooded knoll with an east-west slope overlooking a quiet pond—allowed the placing of the entry at the center of the essentially rectangular plan, on the middle level of the three floors. Entering at this living room level, one walks up seven risers to the bedrooms, or down seven steps to the kitchen–dining area, which in turn opens onto a garden

terrace. Floor-to-ceiling glass, the shed roof, and the absence of full partitions make the house appear more spacious than its dimensions suggest. An 8-foot structural module was maintained throughout. Exterior walls are vertical redwood siding stained gray with creosote bleach; fascias and window and door frames are painted white. The simple shed form of the house was conceived as resting among the tall pine trees, its low profile emphasizing their height.

1 view from the south
2 dining area
3 section
4 main-floor plan
5 upper-level plan

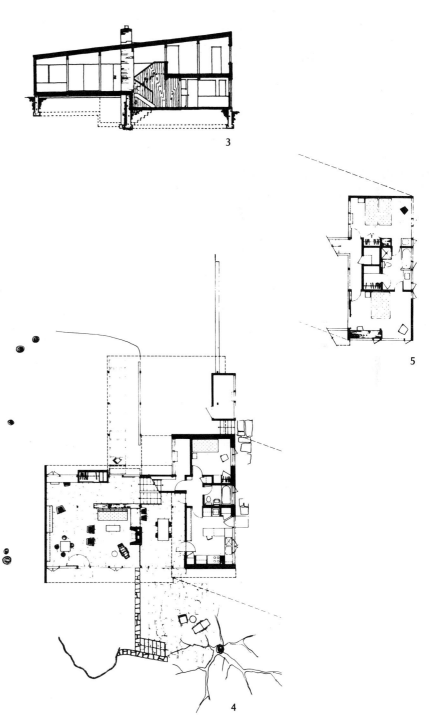

3

5

4

2

65

1

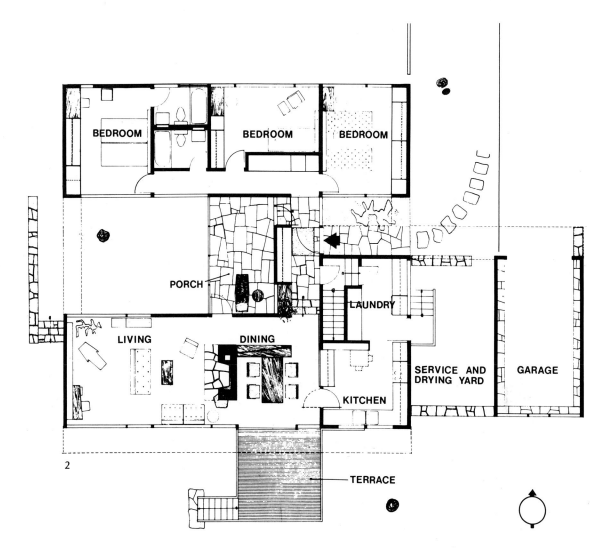

1 overall view
2 plan
3 interior

BEDROOM

BEDROOM

BEDROOM

PORCH

LAUNDRY

LIVING

DINING

SERVICE AND
DRYING YARD

GARAGE

KITCHEN

2

TERRACE

Libby-Owens-Ford Research House, 1945

Part of a building materials research program, this house was designed to exploit an aluminum sandwich wall panel. Corrosion and vermin proof, textured where desirable, colored inside and out, the material could be perforated on one side, when appropriate, for sound absorption. An early example of a prefabricated single interior/exterior wall formation, the panel was not manufactured at the time and has only comparatively recently reached the market.

The plan is binuclear, with an entrance in the hallway that connects the living and sleeping areas. In between is a private terrace, protected from the wind. The fireplace screens the dining area while retaining the overall visual space essential in a small house.

3

Segal House, 1950

A modern and more sophisticated interpretation of the suburban bungalow made good and economical use of a narrow lot. The garage, placed where the front porch would traditionally be, acts as a buffer between the street and living areas. Continuation of the full roof width and overhangs and glazing of the gable end result in its being considered the most beautiful garage on the street. This device also keeps snow shoveling at a minimum. The house's placement to one side of the lot gives two of the bedrooms views across the lawn. Two small interior courts cutting through the roof—one between the entry and the living room and the other separating the dining area from the bedroom wing—bring extra light and a feeling of spaciousness to the interiors. A concrete block grille screening the lawn from the road is another device for seclusion in suburbia. Exterior walls are narrow, vertical redwood siding with accents of white trim. The round steel columns inside the house are wrapped in rope to soften their impact.

1

2

3

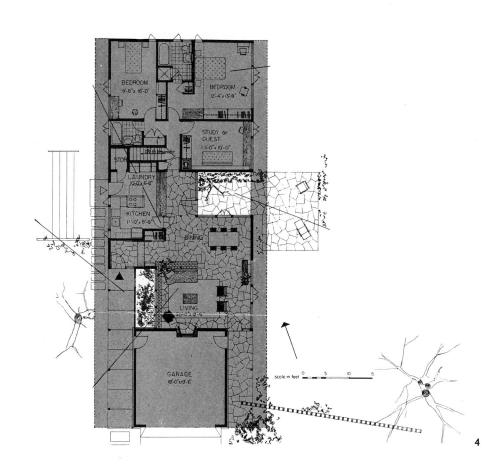

1 view from garden
2 view from street
3 interior
4 plan

4

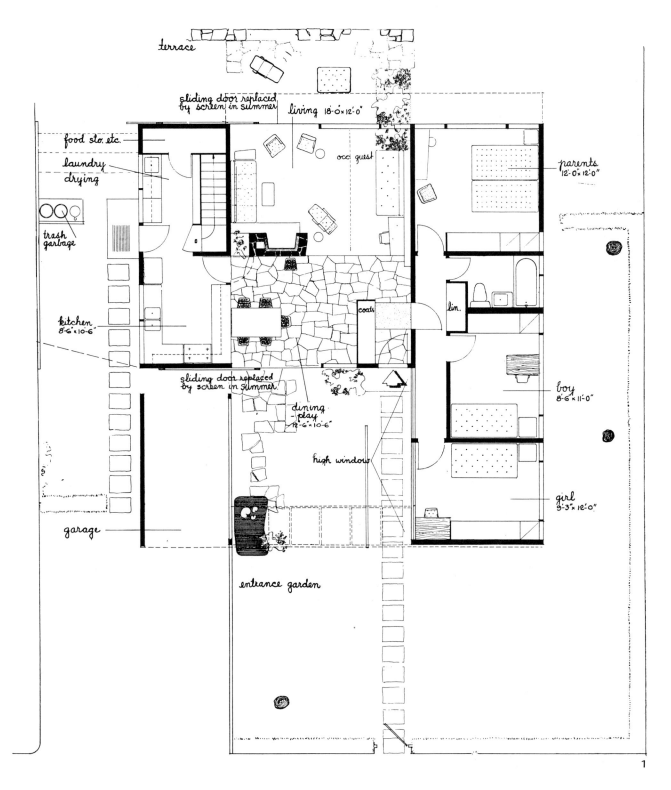

terrace

sliding door replaced by screen in summer

living 18'-0"x12'-0"

occ guest

food sto. etc.

laundry drying

parents 12'-0"x12'-0"

trash garbage

kitchen 8'-6"x10'-6"

coats

lin.

sliding door replaced by screen in summer

dining -play 12'-6"x10'-6"

boy 8'-6"x11'-0"

high window

garage

girl 9'-3"x12'-0"

entrance garden

1

1   plan
2   perspective view by Hugh Stubbins
3   south elevation
4   east elevation
5   site plan
6   presentation

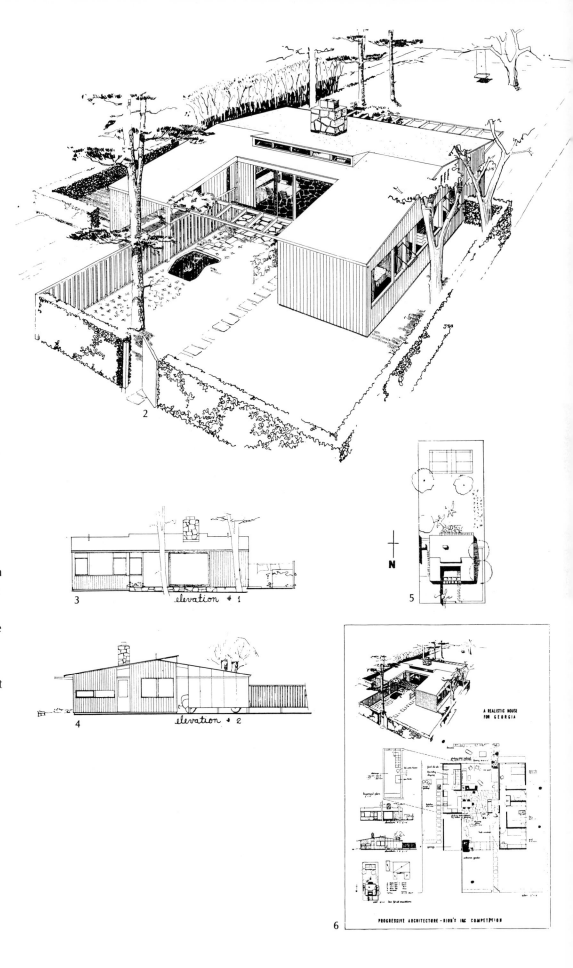

Georgia Builds Competition House, 1945

A national competition held in 1946 by Rich's, Inc., of Atlanta in conjunction with *Progressive Architecture* magazine called for a "realistic house" for a young couple with two children living in Georgia on an annual income of $3000. This little house won first prize and, from a distance of almost 30 years, it may be interesting to quote the opinion of the jury. "First prize went to this very excellent one-story house which conforms so admirably to Georgia's climate and customs. The exterior appearance of this house is charming, and would fit into any Georgia scene. it is nicely located on the lot, and occupies a relatively small portion of the property. Its entrance is near the bedroom wing, yet convenient to the living areas. The living room is divided into three parts—a portion with a view of the back garden, a dining section which overlooks a semi-enclosed court, and a guest-room which can be curtained for privacy. Two of the bedrooms have excellent cross-ventilation, and all have compact built-in features. There is bulk storage space in the basement, within easy access of the service entrance. The garage adjoins the house for convenience. Here is the house our judges believed to be best suited to the needs of a small family in Georgia."

1

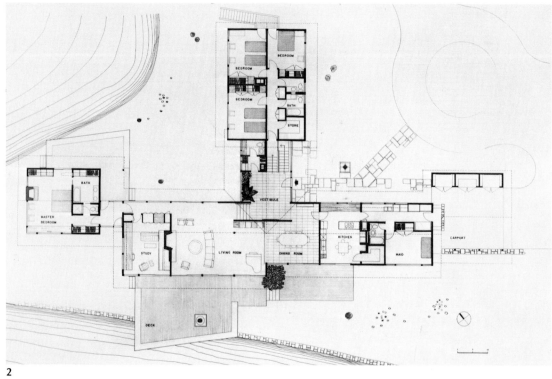

2

1 view from pond
2 plan
3 living room and dining
4 environment

Sharpe House, 1955

Designed for a spit of wooded land projecting into a small lake, this family house is divided into distinct zones to allow privacy and freedom for individual as well as family activities and expansive space for entertaining. The two-story children's wing, separated by the entry from the rest of the house, has bedrooms over a workspace below. A link gives the master suite complete autonomy at one end of the plan.
Both the master suite and the living room have wooden decks hovering over the ground and the water. The vestibule and dining room floors are marble with a genuine Roman mosaic embedded in the hall.

Of post-and-beam construction, the house makes quite dramatic use of fixed and sliding glass to exploit the surrounding water and woodland. This quality of transparency, combined with the low profile and staggered plan, help the house blend with the landscape. In the two-level living and dining area, the wooden ceiling follows the pitch of the roof. This enhances the sense of space, at the same time symbolizing shelter.

3

4

1

Stubbins' House (Cambridge), 1965

Regionalism in architecture has always appealed to me—despite mass production and sophisticated interregional transport and communication. A fascination with barns in New England is freely expressed in the design of my own house in Cambridge. Since the house was designed and built after my children were grown, I was spared the necessity of providing a large number of separate rooms. Instead, I thought of it more as an apartment than a house, a sort of one-room building like a barn with lofts.

This barn influence is evident in the structure as well as the space. I used a form of exposed post-and-beam construction,

with dropped girts, at the exterior walls. Piercing the shell with skylights, projecting windows, and fixed and sliding glass panels—that relate the interior to carefully considered views and access to the outdoors—allows the sun to penetrate the house from different angles during the day.

The corner lot on Brattle Street among stately traditional houses demanded a sympathetic and compatible palette of materials and use of the site. Brick walls screen the house from the street, creating a walled garden in which there is a completely private swimming pool. Extending the brick wall inside the house repeats a favorite detail from houses designed many years ago, a garden corner in the living room. Douglas fir framing, gray-bleached redwood exterior walls and fences, and weathered brick garden walls are all in the local vernacular.

This integration of old and new ideas and materials has been well described by Ziegfeld and Faulkner in their book *Art Today*.

"In the New England tradition are the simple rectangular mass of the house, the double-pitched shingled roof, and the exterior walls of wood. The interior space that reaches to the ceiling, the loftlike bedrooms, and the frankly exposed structure are reminiscent of New England barns. Strictly contemporary are the living room wall of fixed and sliding glass and the varied windows that are placed where needed rather than in a stereotyped formal arrangement.

The group-living area is an intriguing, multidimensional composition that combines great freedom of spatial movement with a reassuring sense of substantial architectural enclosure. Built of dark-red brick, the 26-foot chimney

accentuates the loftiness of the room. The low-ceilinged entrance–dining area and the study are inviting havens. Contrasting materials emphasize the size and shape of the space. Walls and ceilings of rough plaster painted white accentuate the darker elements and make the room light and airy. Dark, reddish-brown tiles, similar in color to the bricks of the fireplace, are used on the floor of the entrance–dining area. Traditional, random-width oak boards are a quiet background for the large Oriental rug intricately patterned in dark reds, blues and white. A chair, an ottoman, and sofas upholstered in white, and a natural wood chair and tables, are arranged in an open yet sociable conversation group."

Designing every detail of the house and most of the furniture and closely supervising construction were particular pleasures at a time when the practice had grown too large to make house design economically viable. It brought home to me how central to my development as an architect are strong roots in house design.

2

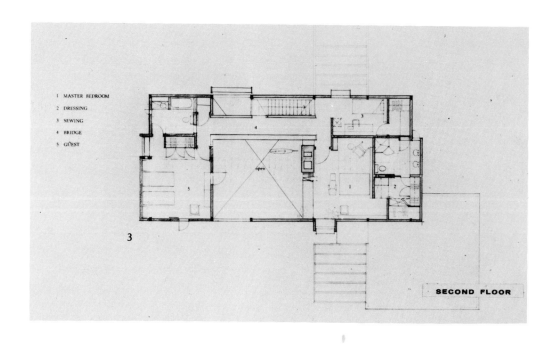

1 MASTER BEDROOM
2 DRESSING
3 SEWING
4 BRIDGE
5 GUEST

3

SECOND FLOOR

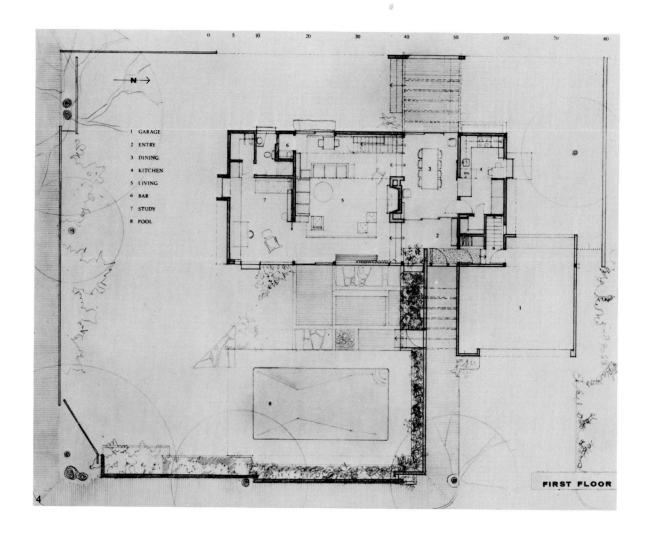

1 GARAGE
2 ENTRY
3 DINING
4 KITCHEN
5 LIVING
6 BAR
7 STUDY
8 POOL

N →

4

FIRST FLOOR

5

7

6

8

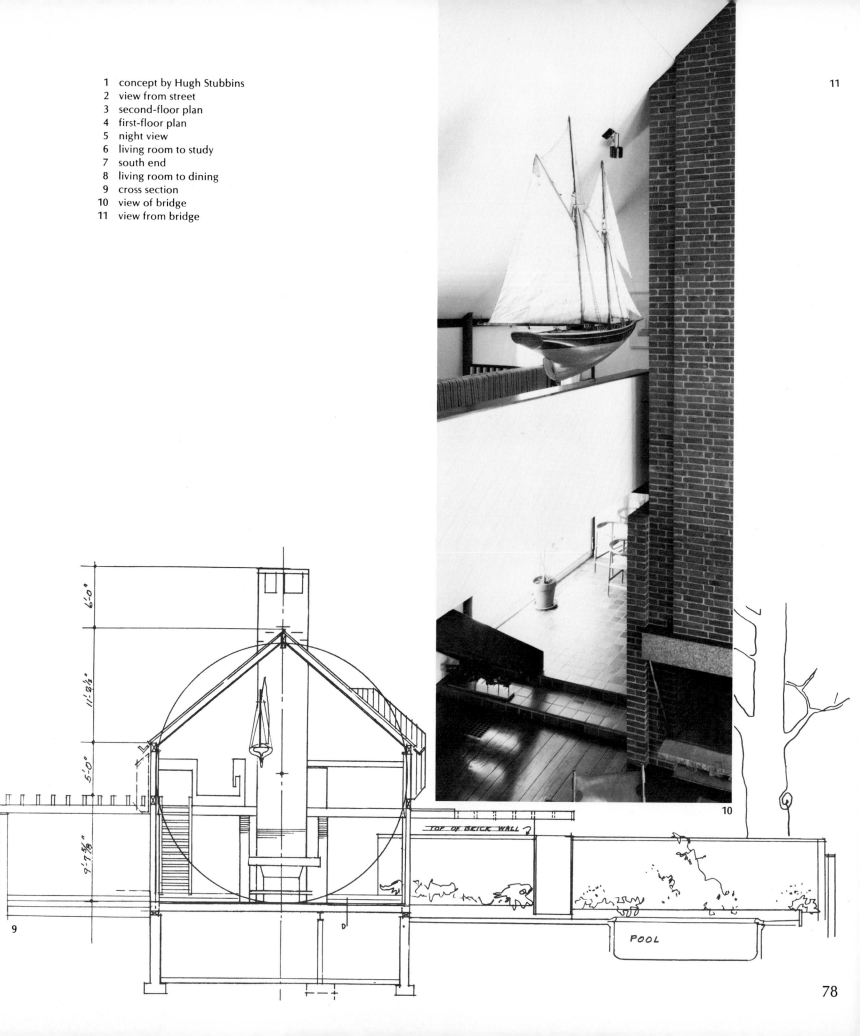

10

9

TOP OF BRICK WALL

POOL

Housing

Despite our emotional attachment as a nation to the private house as dwelling place, the reality of many people's lives is, and will continue to be, something different. City dwellers live in apartments or housing projects; students—many of them—still live in dormitories; and row houses and condominiums are competing with the single-family home in a number of rural and suburban communities.

Yet even in this high-density life-style many of the same emotional demands are made. People still want a sense of place. Privacy, identity, and security become even more important.

The architect's challenge is to provide all these elements in an economically and physically viable solution. Some ways to achieve this are through circulation—small elevator lobbies, broken corridors, separate entrances, and screened yards or porches. Proper acoustical control, articulation of the individual unit within the overall scheme, and some flexibility of plan arrangement are other devices for giving people the essential identity they need.

When the American campus was going through a period of upheaval and dormitory living became unpopular, this lesson was vividly brought home to us. We found that the opportunity for personal modification of the environment greatly improved the morale of the students, their reaction to their dormitories, and their treatment of them. The same lesson has been learned in a number of public housing projects. Hostility—sometimes expressed in vandalism or at least sloppy maintenance—could be channeled into creative energy if the building design and management would permit the possibility of handmade furniture, colored walls, a choice of floor coverings, and modification of lighting.

Understanding how people feel about the places they live in is an essential but difficult part of the architectural process. It demands some humility and restraint in resisting the temptation to design buildings that demand too much conformity from their occupants.

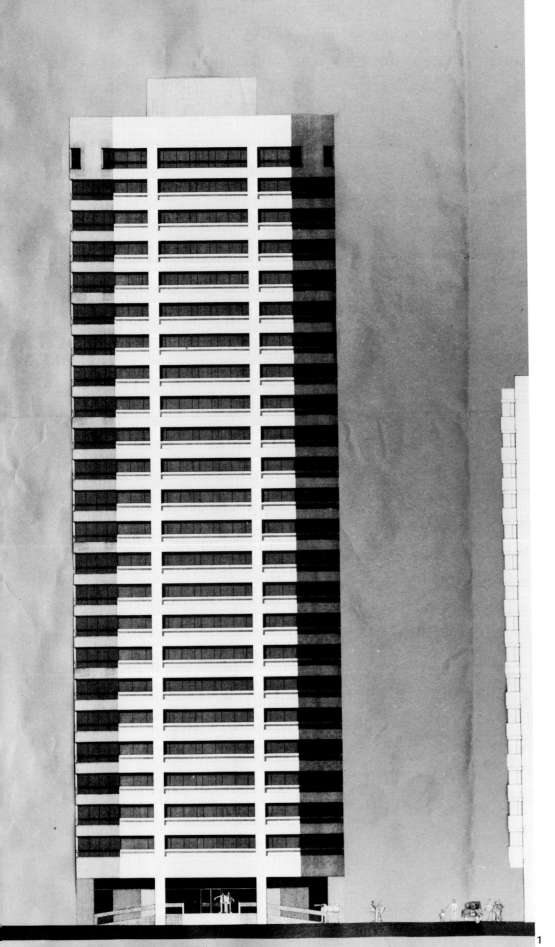

EAST ELEVATION

1

MIT Graduate Student Housing, Cambridge, 1969

A square plan with chamfered corners and a central service core achieved the equivalent of eight corner rooms per floor to give each of eight apartments a living room with a panoramic view. Designed originally for 400 graduate students living two or three to an apartment, the flexible arrangement of the floor plan makes it easy to convert from single to married student housing. A student committee participated in the design process from the beginning and was influential in the choice of the final scheme from a number of alternatives. A full-scale mock-up of a typical apartment was prepared, and questionnaires, distributed to all potential residents, elicited a lively response.

A special precast concrete and steel structural system was developed for this 24-story building. Perimeter spandrel and column assemblies—precast offsite as single components and stacked vertically a floor at a time—were used with steel framing for the central core of the structure. The floor system of 8-inch-deep precast concrete floor planks with 2-inch concrete topping made for structural consistency. This structural design of the enclosing wall and floor system eliminated the need for diagonal wind bracing or moment-resisting connections and also achieved some economy over traditional techniques.

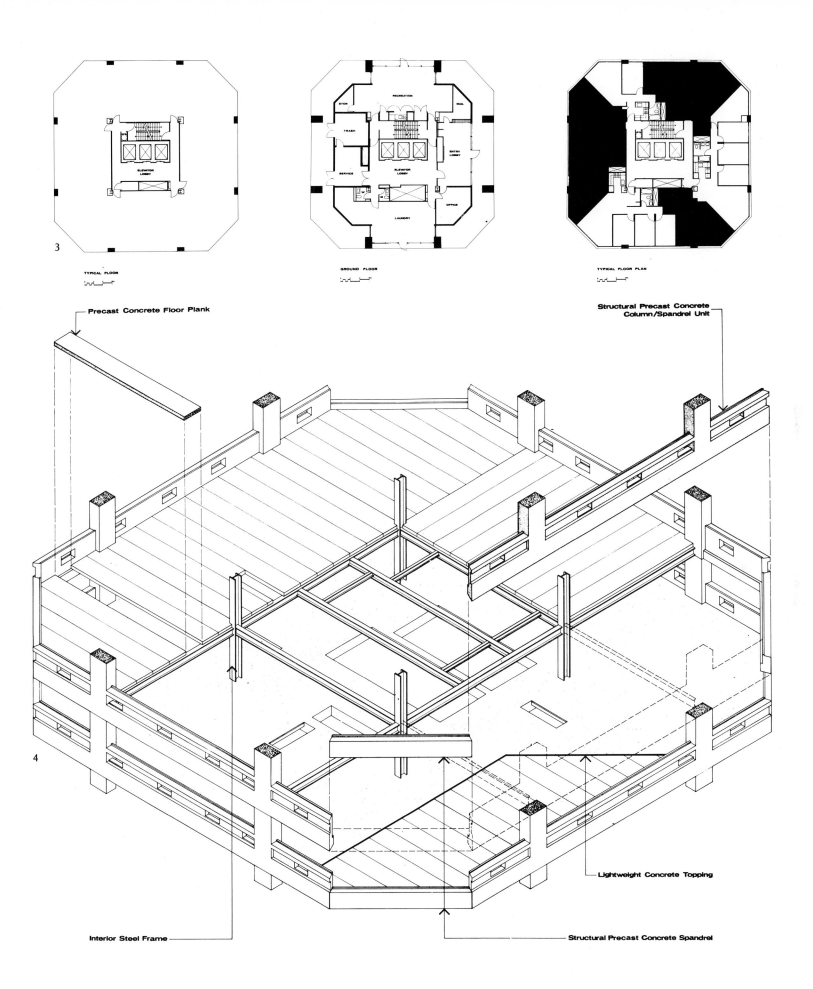

3

TYPICAL FLOOR

GROUND FLOOR

TYPICAL FLOOR PLAN

Precast Concrete Floor Plank

Structural Precast Concrete
Column/Spandrel Unit

4

Lightweight Concrete Topping

Interior Steel Frame

Structural Precast Concrete Spandrel

1

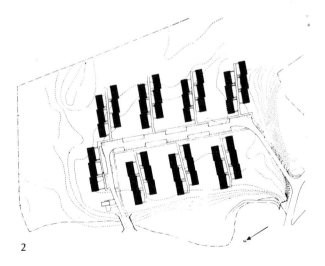

2

Wellesley Veterans' Housing, 1948

The staggered site plan affords private entrances to each of the 90 units in this low-cost housing development while breaking the monotony of the typical row configuration. Two- and three-bedroom units are grouped in pairs—three pairs constituting a six-unit building. The 15 buildings are placed endwise to the main access road to give added quiet and privacy to living areas. The staggered row formation allows full exploitation of the 15-acre site to provide ample courts between each group. Planting in the middle of each court screens the view from opposing glass-walled living rooms. Street facades are shielded behind perforated cinder block garden walls, which also establish private areas for drying

1 general view
2 site plan
3 two-bedroom plan
4 three-bedroom plan
5 entrance detail
6 environment
7 perspective
8 entry lane

5

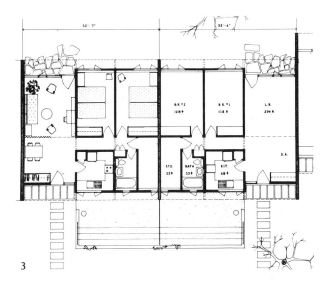

3

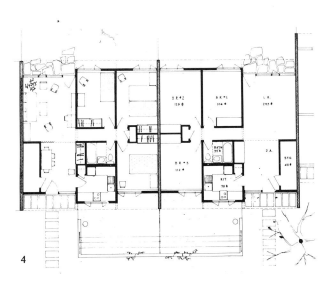

4

6

clothes or other "backyard" activities. To avoid the hot western sun, dwellings are oriented either to the north or south. Those facing north have south clerestories over living rooms and bathrooms to admit some sunlight for warming color. All apartments have radiant heating, and, since they lack basements, each is provided with an ample interior storage room.

7

8

1

Brookline Farm Development, 1958

The serpentine configuration of this proposed 652-unit private housing project was conceived as a means of inviting expansion of the surrounding parkland right into the wide crescent area formed by the two buildings. Although it would be privately owned and maintained, the land around the buildings was also intended for the use of nearby residents for passive recreation and view. Because the site overlooks the lakes and lagoons of a Brookline greenbelt area known as the Riverway, the buildings are oriented to the southeast to give each apartment the advantage of the view and the sunlight.

Two-level parking built into the hillside at the rear of the larger building was planned to free as much of the land as possible from the intrusion of the automobile. Apartment access corridors—placed on the side of the building away from the park view on alternate floors—are connected via stairways with the units above and below. This arrangement has the bonus of allowing most of the apartments to extend the full depth of the building with exposures at both ends. All living rooms face the view. The low building height is consistent with the surrounding residential neighborhood.

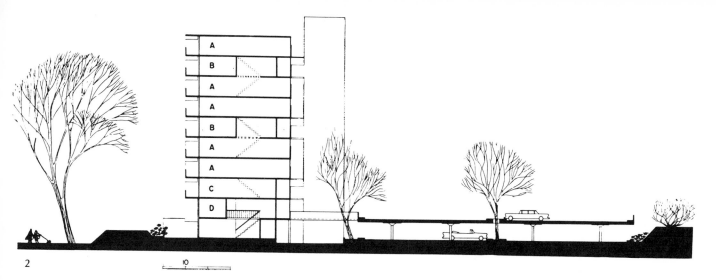

2

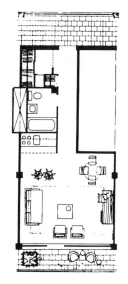

1 overall view, model
2 cross section
3 plans
4 interior view
5 site plan, model

A. ONE BEDROOM   A. TWO BEDROOM   B. EFFICIENCY

3

4

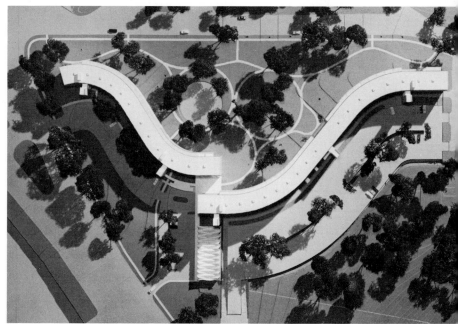

5

Warren Gardens Low-Income Housing, Boston, 1964

A hilly and rocky site, which posed a number of structural and design problems, turned out in the end to be an advantage. This made it possible to fit the buildings unobtrusively into the hillside and to landscape the spaces in between, giving a variety of opportunities for walking, children's playing, or just sitting in the shade. The passages between buildings become shortcuts from one group to the other, so lacking in the grid-dominated urban scene.

The 229 low-income housing units, designed in association with Ashley, Myer, and Associates, were conceived as townhouses rather in the idiom of the English semidetached row house, each with its own small garden. To get away from the much disliked "project look," particular care was exercised in the detailing of the clapboard and concrete masonry exteriors, the masonry units being used as firewalls to relieve the "endless" quality of row house construction. These further define the individual dwellings and provide an effective sound barrier between them.

The majority of the units are planned as two- and three-bedroom townhouses, some combining an efficiency apartment on the lower level, with duplexes above.

2

3

1 detail view
2 general view
3 site plan

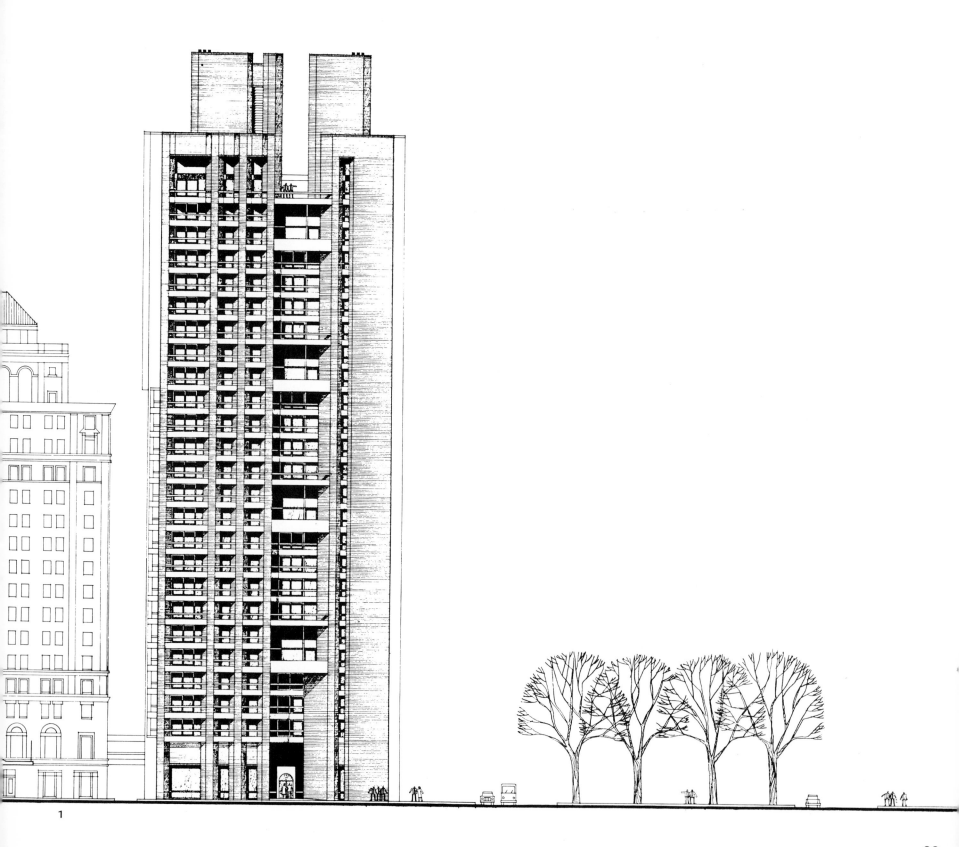

1

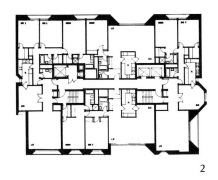

2

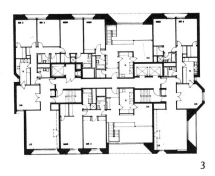

3

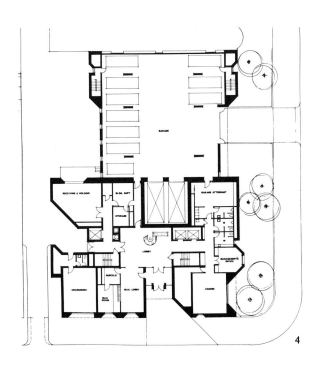

4

Carlton House, Boston, 1964

A luxury apartment tower—located right on the edge of the Boston Public Gardens—was planned to form a gateway terminating Commonwealth Avenue. When this building was planned, it was anticipated that another, similar tower would be built on the opposite side of the avenue to complete the gateway effect.

The reinforced concrete structure was designed to contain large luxury apartments of varying types that could be personalized or individualized to create elegant and distinctive suites and two spectacular penthouses. All would have views either of the gardens or out over Back Bay. A direct connection was planned with the neighboring Ritz Hotel so that special services could be provided to residents. Unfortunately, it was never built!

1   elevation facing public garden
2,3   typical plans
4   groundfloor plan

330 Beacon Street, Boston, 1955

The unusual feature of this apartment tower is that the living rooms of all apartments face the Charles River Basin. This was accomplished by using three elevator cores, each of which serves two apartments per floor. The possibility of elevator breakdowns and repairs being taken into account, these elevator cores are connected by a corridor on every third floor. Residents thus have only to walk up or down one flight to regain elevator service. This core arrangement also gives an unusual feeling of privacy in an apartment building, since only two suites open off each lobby. Living rooms are large, with sliding glass doors opening to balconies that exploit the views.

Since the land in Back Bay is man-made, the 155-foot-high building is founded on concrete piling extending to bedrock 240 feet below the ground.

1 view from street
2 typical above-and-below-corridor floor plan
3 typical corridor floor plan
4 living room

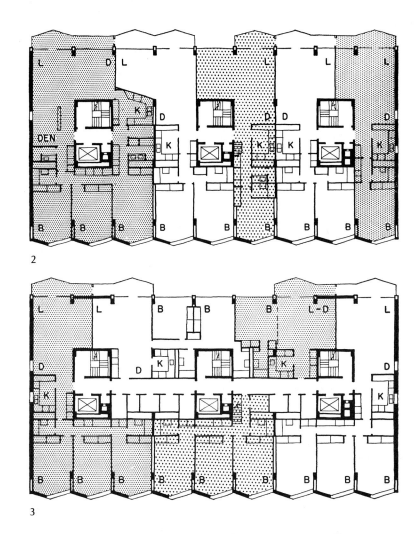

95

Campus Architecture

In the last few decades the American campus has been the scene of unrepressed architectural virtuosity. A receptive client, a serene and homogeneous environment, a youthful and exuberant user group—perhaps approximating most closely in the modern era to the patron of the past—have called forth architectural gymnastics. And virtuosity on the campus is not always out of place. Monumental neoclassical or gothic buildings may demand some counterstatement from their modern neighbors. There is no intrinsic reason why a new building should recede into the background to allow the old campus to hold sway in a new era of educational techniques and student life-styles. Yet, because the campus environment is venerated and historic, even an assertive new building should respect the character of what is there. We crave homogeneity today and have so little of it that we should treat with care what still remains.

Additions to the campus must be framed by the parameters set by college budgets, student life-styles, and a continuity between past and future that is, after all, at the heart of campus life—the theme of recurring youth against a background of age, even if the current generation of students is too close to itself to acknowledge this or too antagonistic to its immediate forebears to admit its relationship to them. This continuity is important and should inhibit us from placing a new member of the physical environment into a context with which it is out of sympathy. Materials, massing, use of the site, rooflines, and building height are all devices by which a new building may be on speaking terms with its neighbors without in any way imitating the design philosophy or construction techniques of previous generations.

Sometimes, as in the venerated Harvard Yard, where we are designing a new library, the "completeness" of the existing environment does indeed demand a nonbuilding. In this case we have taken our cue and gone underground.

1

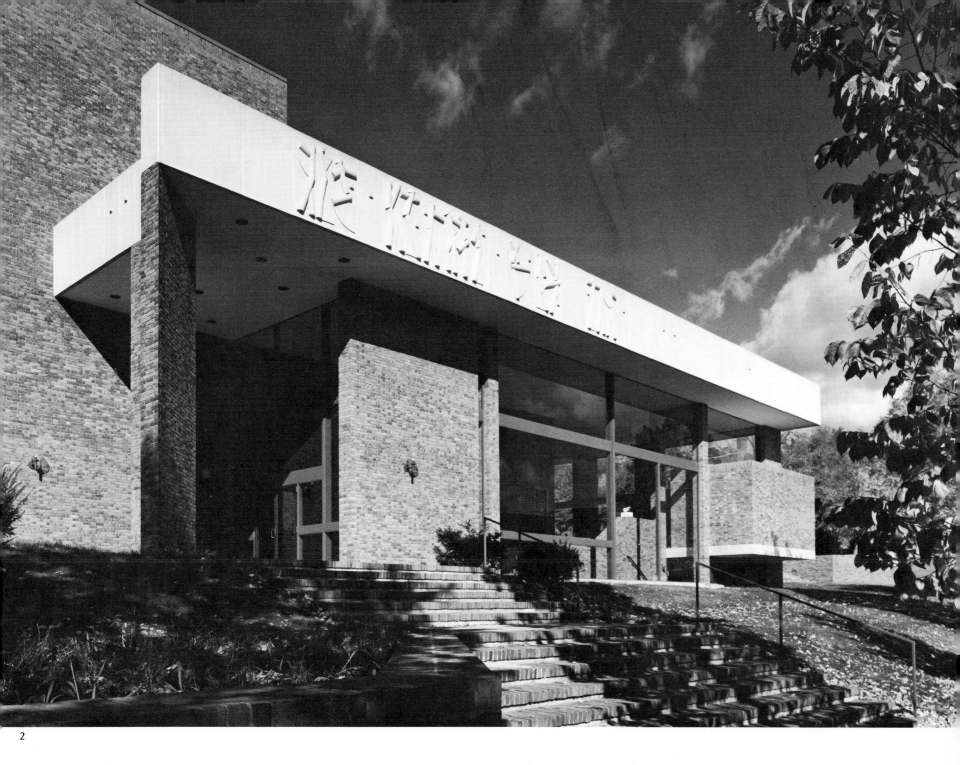

2

Mount Holyoke College Laboratory Theater, Massachusetts, 1964

Because the primary purpose of this theater is the teaching of theater arts and speech, it is oriented toward the campus, the student entrance being connected to the campus walk system. But because the theater department presents several shows a year to the public, theatergoers also have their own approach to the building under a portico embracing the high wall of the stagehouse.

1   perspective by Hugh Stubbins
2   principal entrance and main facade

3

4
5

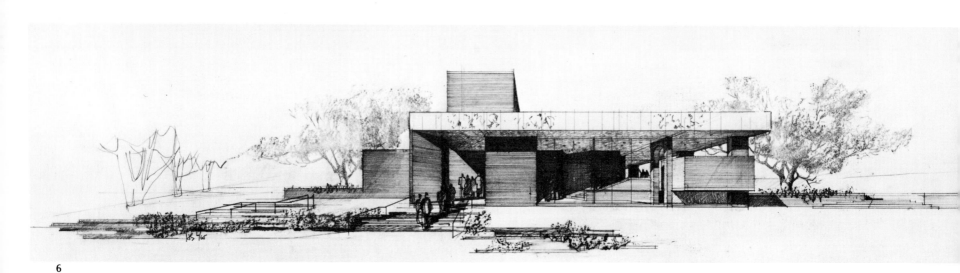

6

This route to the auditorium leads one through an interesting variety of spatial volumes. The sense of height lessens as one passes from the high-ceilinged ticket foyer into the lobby and goes up the stairs to the coat check area. Then, turning 180 degrees through the upper lobby, one enters the auditorium under the lower ceiling created by the control booth above. Once one is inside the auditorium, the space again expands.

The intent is to heighten the theatergoer's sense of anticipation by the variety of experiences along the way. He will have been gradually transported into an environment that will release his imagination, not capture it.

On the secluded west side of the auditorium are two levels of teaching spaces, comprising design room, costume-making room, speech–radio studio, and faculty offices. Here, and in the workshop to the rear of the stage, the major activity takes place. Its separate entrance permits student traffic to be segregated from public functions. Public areas may be closed off without affecting the teaching function of the building.

The functional relationship of the educational area and the public domain are like two hooks joined together. The producers and actors meet the public at the stage.

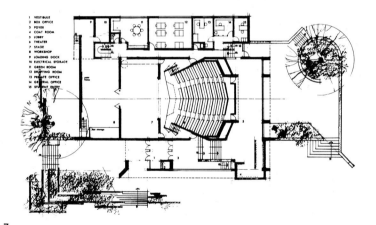

7

9

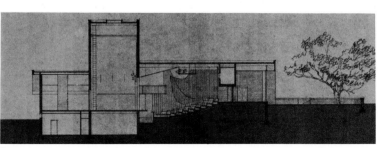

8

3 entrance detail
4 theater
5 lobby
6 concept sketch by Hugh Stubbins
7 plan
8 section
9 entrance detail

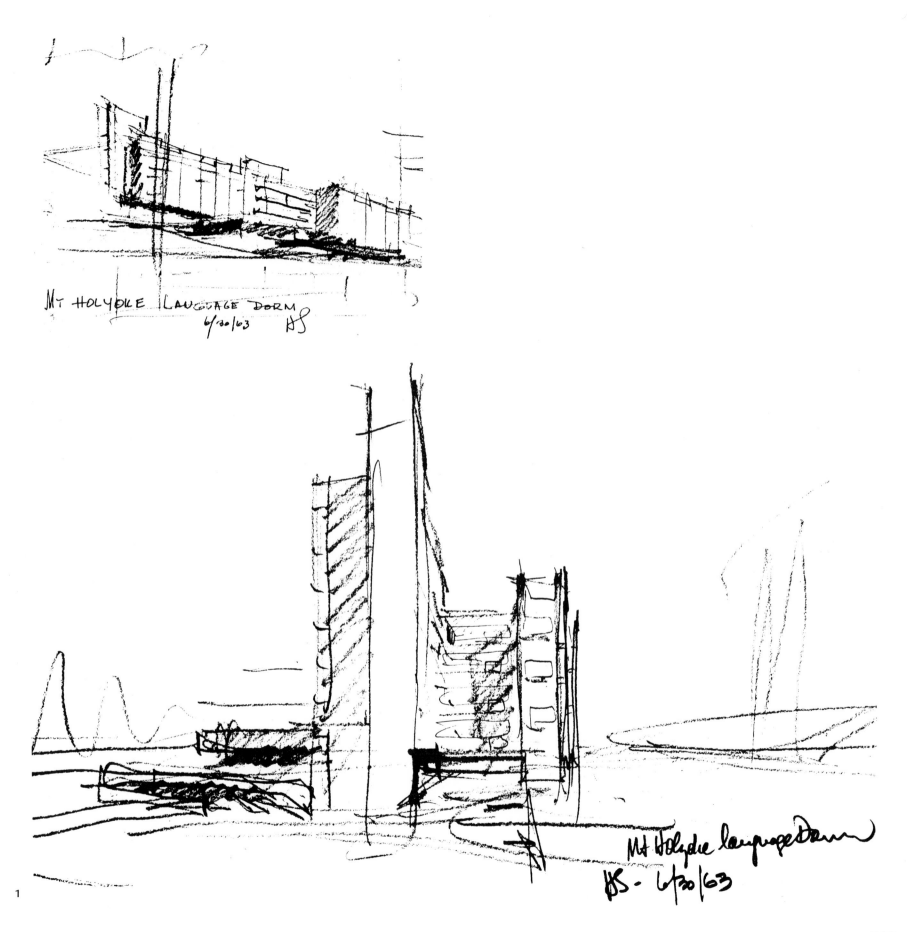

MT HOLYOKE LANGUAGE DORM
6/30/63 HS

Mt Holyoke language Dorm
HS - 6/30/63

1

2

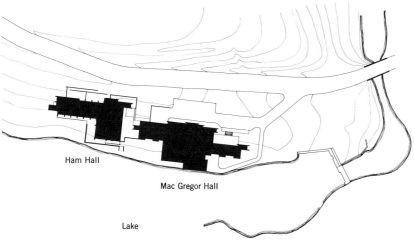

Ham Hall

Mac Gregor Hall

Lake

3

Mount Holyoke College Dormitories, 1962–1964

The Mount Holyoke campus is a relatively homogeneous collection of buildings predominantly in the neogothic style—with masonry the dominant material. Respecting the character and atmosphere of the campus, the new buildings have exterior walls of waterstruck brick and strongly expressed vertical elements.

The sloping lakeside site was exploited to join two residence halls, allowing them to share one kitchen and service point but also giving each building its own identity. Siting of the buildings was carefully studied to make sure that the wooded countryside, peaceful rural views, and serene, traditional campus atmosphere were disturbed as little as possible.

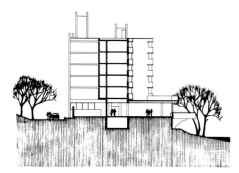

4

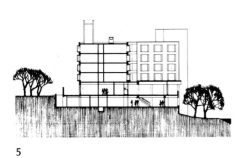

5

6

7

Ham and McGregor Halls between them house 250 students in single and double rooms. Ham Hall, the college's "Language House," makes use of a single-loaded corridor to give all students views over the lake. McGregor uses both single- and double-loaded corridors—balancing the advantages of lakeside views from bay-windowed double rooms against the privacy of singles on the opposite side. Each floor has its own lounge with appropriate utility rooms.

At the entry level, each building has a spacious lounge with a fireplace and windows overlooking the lake. There are also smaller, more intimate lounges and apartments for faculty members. Dining rooms on the lower levels, convenient to the kitchen, take advantage of the lake view by means of cantilevered balconies.

The structure for both buildings is reinforced-concrete, flat-slab construction with masonry cavity walls. All interior walls—except in the service areas—are surfaced with plaster, wood, or tile.

8

Mount Holyoke College Art Building, 1966

The Art Building is organized as a two-story teaching facility standing over a one-story museum.

Its length placed at right angles to a steeply sloping site, the building connects and is entered from two levels. A bridge at the upper road level, adjacent to other academic buildings, serves as the main classroom–studio entrance. The lower level entry to the museum and auditorium is appropriately located between two features of the campus, the Gettell Amphitheater and the Class of 1904 Garden, all frequented by campus visitors as well as students.

The lower level exhibition lobby gives direct access to the auditorium and to the museum. Designed for college films as well as lectures, the 400-seat auditorium can be divided into two self-contained rooms seating 100 and 300 people. The museum—also accessible from the lower lobby—contains four galleries for the college's permanent collection, as well as large, flexible space for special exhibitions, and an outdoor sculpture garden.

Between the active top floor and the first floor museum are the quieter art department facilities—photography and slide room, seminar room, department library, faculty offices, and lounges—all of which have views of the garden and the amphitheater.

The structure is cast-in-place concrete with tubular columns and flat slab floors. The exterior waterstruck-brick infill walls harmonize with the rest of the campus. Changes in fenestration and a strongly articulated structure express functional changes at the different levels within the building.

1 lower-level entrance
2 site plan
3 upper-level plan
4 middle-level plan
5 groundfloor plan

3

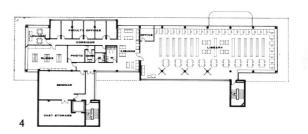

4

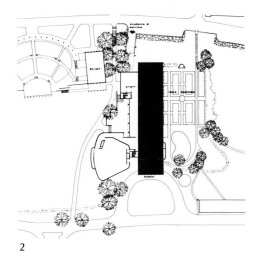

2

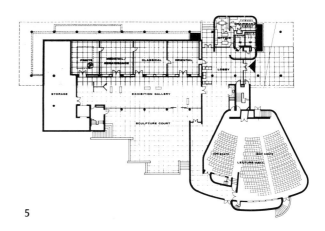

5

6

6 upper-level entrance, sketch by Hugh Stubbins III
7 upper-level entrance
8 elevation from the north
9 courtyard
10 library

7

8

9

10

University of Massachusetts, 1962–66

In the early 1960s the University of Massachusetts had to plan for dramatic expansion of its Amherst campus to accommodate a rapid increase in student enrollment. Having acquired in 1963 a 35-acre tract of farmland south and west of the existing campus, the university commissioned us to plan and design a complex of housing and dining facilities for about 6000 students to be known as the Southwest Quadrangle.

The bold and somewhat controversial decision to introduce five 22-story towers into the rural scene was almost inevitable. Without the towers, the development would have spread out into the countryside, making distances between buildings excessive and difficult for students to negotiate within the university timetable. In fact, the towers have become quite a dramatic feature of the scenery, clearly visible from Route 9 between Amherst and Northampton. They take on a more personal character as one approaches the quadrangle and walks among the buildings. Their relationship to the low-rise buildings and the variety of spatial experiences provided by the landscaped walks and spaces in between have softened the impact of urban scale upon the expansive farmland of the Connecticut River Valley.

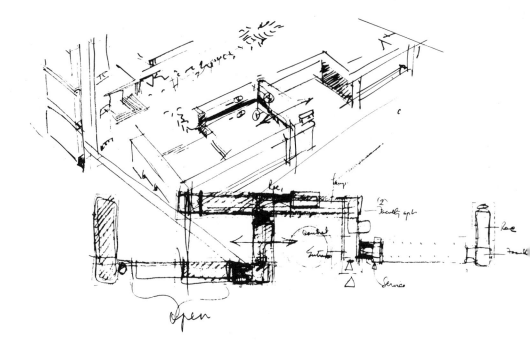

1

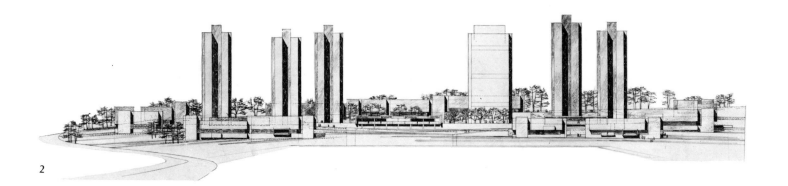

2

3

1 concept sketches by Hugh Stubbins
2 concept elevation
3 aerial view
4 cross section

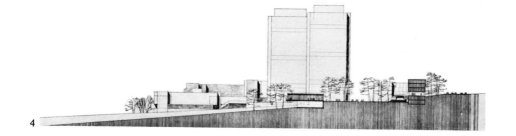

4

5   high and low rise on sloping terrain
6   site plan
7   "Propylaeum" main entrance

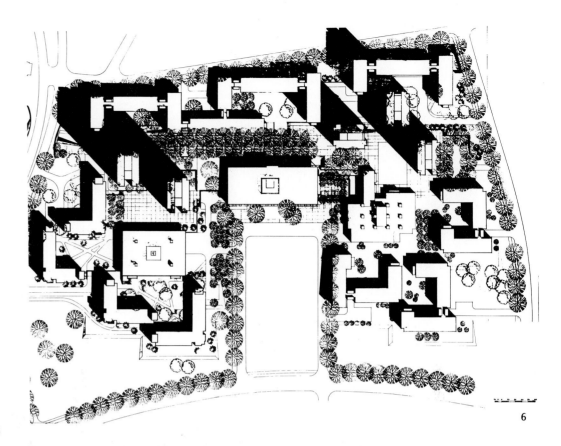

6

In addition to the high-rise buildings, the quadrangle consists of 11 low-rise residential halls and 3 dining commons. The complex was built over a period of 4 years, and construction was carefully phased to ensure that appropriate dining facilities were ready for use in time to serve each stage of the construction.

The plan for the site revolves around a mall or pedestrian spine defining an asymmetric axis to which all buildings in the quadrangle have access, with clear connections through to the main campus.

The site plan provides a variety of sheltered courts at different levels—important in an area where the winter climate can be harsh, the wind strong, and the sun something to be captured and savored. The multilevel courts are linked together by ramps and steps. Buildings along the eastern boundary of the quadrangle have access to one of the town streets as well as to the internal pedestrian mall. Several small parking areas introduced along the surrounding streets are for the use of resident faculty, graduate students, visitors, and service personnel.

The low-rise dormitories, which range in height from three to six stories, have a ground-level public floor containing a reception area, lounges, meeting rooms, and a special apartment for the "head of the house" or supervisor. Above this, dormitory floors are planned to include a majority of

7

8

9

8   dining commons interior detail
9   dining commons and mall
10   environmental view

two-person rooms, with some single- and four-person suites interspersed. Each floor has a lounge and common study area. The towers are similarly organized, the equivalent of three "houses" being stacked vertically. Thus six dormitory floors share a lounge floor inserted in the middle of the sandwich.

The structural system for all the buildings is reinforced cast-in-place concrete utilizing a double cantilever framing. Face brick and concrete block infill are employed for exterior walls. The pattern of fenestration is designed to treat large wall areas as a single plane. The windows are randomly placed, producing an element of variety in otherwise similar rooms and constituting neither a vertical nor horizontal pattern. Inside, resilient tile was used for all student living area floors, with carpet in the lounges and corridors.

The strong architectural expression of structure and materials, softened by landscaping and more gentle, intimate detailing, aims to give the students the exhilaration that comes from bold forms and spaces, as well as the security derived from human scale and defined circulation patterns. The dining commons were planned to go beyond food and snack service to create an environment for relaxation and discussion—making mealtimes the focus of informal social and cultural exchanges among faculty, students, and visitors.

10

1

Francis A. Countway Library of Medicine
Boston, 1961

Countway was the first library we designed. But, curiously enough, lack of library experience was a positive factor in getting the job, for the building committee felt it would guarantee an open-minded approach to its carefully developed program.

Containing as it does the collection of the Harvard Medical School and the Boston Medical Library and acting as a central resource for the entire medical community, Countway is one of the largest and most important medical libraries in the country. This fact, plus its setting amid the monumental, neoclassical buildings of the Harvard Medical School, suggested the concept of a modern building with sufficient strength of its own to stand up to its neighbors without being overpowered. At the same time, we recognized the need for harmony between the old and new. This consideration determined the building height, the use of limestone to blend with the rather poor grade of marble of the older buildings, the alignment and bold expression of the top floor "cornice," and the manipulation of shadow to suggest—in reverse image—the plastic strength of the projecting columns and cornices of neoclassical forms.

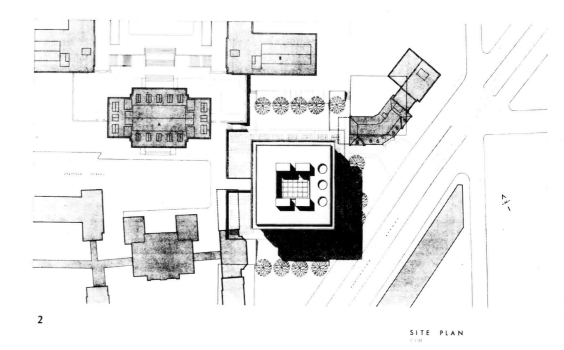

2

SITE PLAN

3

1 entrance facade and its surroundings
2 site plan
3 elevation relationship
4 view from courtyard
5 monumental stair

115

Despite their grand and monumental appearance, the older buildings have a system of small, well-planned laboratories inside. We wanted, therefore, the new building to establish a different pace and atmosphere—the serene, spacious feeling of an academic living room in which people, doing rigorous theoretical and experimental research, could experience a mental and physical stretching of the legs. This sense of space is achieved by means of large open floors focusing on the open well at the center of the building. This open, central core provides immediate orientation for people in all parts of the building and keeps circulating traffic away from quiet reading rooms located in cantilevered alcoves at the perimeter of the building. Although quiet and secluded, these alcoves are immediately accessible to the open stack floors, and their exposure to outside sunlight is carefully controlled. Designed for flexible use, they can be used as seminar rooms, lounges, and conference rooms, as well as for individual study carrels.

The restricted site and the classic symmetry of the existing buildings almost suggested a square plan and a vertical organization of the functional elements, each of which is clearly articulated in the form of the building. The eight-story building is set in a sunken plaza with two levels below grade. The lowest level expands beneath the brick-paved plaza to connect with service elevators—descending from a glass-box, detached delivery kiosk—and with the series of tunnels linking the entire complex. The symmetry of the building is reinforced by identical treatment of all four elevations. A bridge spanning the plaza leads to the entrance, the circulation desk, and the main lobby.

Sited to form a dramatic visual focus of culmination of avenues through the complex, Countways's presence in the environment will be much enhanced when the planned removal of the existing Peter Bent Brigham Hospital buildings near the entrance forecourt actually takes place.

5

Landscaping, which includes tubbed trees, plants, and shrubs, has the unusual symbolic feature of a scion of Hippocrates' Tree from the Mediterranean Island of Cos, beneath which Hippocrates is said to have held dialogue with his disciples.

At the time Countway was designed, the concept of a vertical solution was regarded somewhat dubiously by librarians, who were accustomed to having all the essential elements on one floor, where they could be easily supervised. We had considerable discussion over control and circulation and seriously studied the question of whether our solution of the open well with adjacent circulation cores would entail more walking for the staff than the more conventional central core. A time and motion study proved that the amount of walking was about the same in both cases.

The composition of a medical library lent itself very well to a vertical solution, for it was possible to separate the two basic elements—journals and monographs (books)—with the main checkout and card catalogue floor in between. Entering at the main level, one goes up for books and monographs and down for periodicals, but both levels are visible from the central control desk and entrance lobby.

The small projecting study carrels—although there is room in them only for a working surface and a chair—have proved very popular and have to be reserved. They seem to provide the desired degree of privacy and quiet without isolation from visual participation in the life of the building as a whole.

Since we were commissioned to design the entire facility—interiors and furnishings as well—it was possible to consider the building a completely integrated whole and use materials and detailing to reinforce the architectural concept and functional requirements. Full-scale mock-ups of part of the building, to which we had considerable response, gave us the benefit of genuine user participation.

Skylights over the central well provide an effective light cap to the interior space but might perhaps have been angled to throw shafts of sunlight down into the well.

Since problems of heat and glare associated with large areas of glass had not been particularly well solved in library buildings at that time, major study floors were oriented to the interior court, with only narrow fenestration in the study alcoves. The main entry floor and the two top floors—which house meeting rooms and the offices of two learned journals—have glass perimeter walls, well protected from sunlight, either by the roof overhang or the alcove projections.

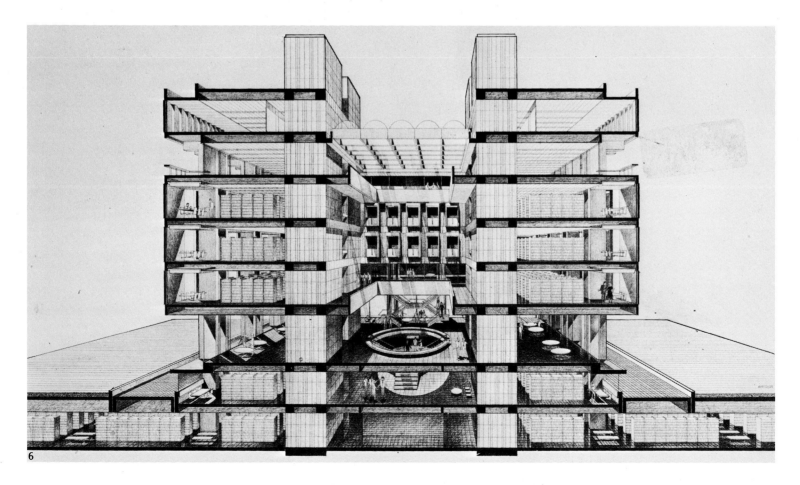

6

6 explanatory section
7 groundfloor lobby

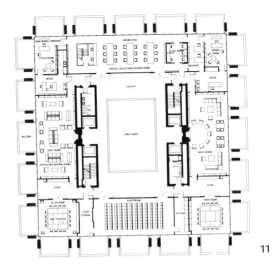

11

8

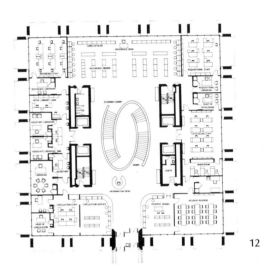

12

9

10

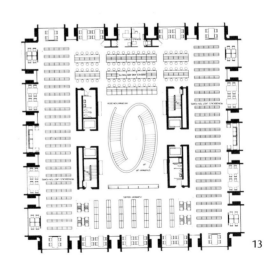

13

120

The meeting rooms on the fifth floor, comfortably furnished with lounge furniture, fireplaces, and memorabilia from the original library collections, are very popular for semisocial functions and informal lectures. This floor has the advantage of balconies formed by the alcove projection of the lower floors. The sixth floor—above the roof of the central core— has outside walls in the center as well as on the perimeter. It is used for rental office space and mechanical equipment.

The structural system for the library is reinforced concrete frame consisting of a beam and flat slab spanning from the outer ring of double columns to the four internal core towers, which provide both vertical support and lateral bracing and thereby produce a column-free interior. All the floor slabs were designed for a uniform live load of 150 pounds per square foot to permit placement of standard bookshelving anywhere within the building. The building is totally air conditioned and humidity controlled by means of a double-duct, steam-driven air system. The high-velocity distribution makes use of main supply and return riser ducts integrated within the four vertical core towers, each distributing to horizontal zones. Air intake at the perimeter is above the ceiling, and the only visible grilles are return air. The integrated ceiling incorporates narrow light fixtures, designed especially for Countway, that have now become standard equipment. All duct systems were designed for low decibel ratings, lined with fiberglass sound-absorbing material, and equipped with down-rated attenuators. The major mechanical components and high-pressure equipment are housed in an underground equipment room located below the paved plaza and adjacent to existing utility lines. Special intake grilles or building "nostrils" receive fresh air near the rim of the forecourt planting area.

14

8 perimeter reader alcove
9 catalogues
10 monumental stair
11 plan, fifth level
12 plan, lower level
13 plan, entrance level
14 interior skylit court

1

Hamilton College Library
Clinton, New York, 1968

Completed in 1972, the library forms the dominant element terminating the main campus quadrangle. The building is approached from the south through a deep undercut portico offering a sheltered gathering point for students, faculty, and visitors. Conceived as a simple, efficient rectangle, the plan is based on a modular stack-bay, 25 feet 6 inches square. Services and vertical circulation elements are held to the perimeter, leaving the center of the building free and flexible and the basic building system open-ended for expansion to the north. The only interior fixed elements are the cylindrical concrete columns and a small elevator near the center serving essential library functions.

Organized on four levels—three above grade—the plan places technical, administrative, and control functions in the west bays of the main floor and basement. The upper floors contain the main collection and reading spaces, which flow around a central, skylit well. Moving through these spaces, one is quickly oriented to the organization and scope of the building and its resources. In general, two-story spaces denote areas for more leisurely reading and informal study. The quiet, private areas are at the perimeter of the building, shielded by a "buffer" of bookstacks.

On the main floor, a one-story projecting room has a dual use. During regular hours it is open to library users for browsing among current periodicals. After hours it can be closed off from the main building to become a self-contained night reading room with its own entry, telephones, and toilets.

The structure is cast-in-place reinforced concrete using a round column with dropped head and flat-slab floor construction. The entire upper structure is surfaced with buff-colored limestone panels with shot-sawn finish. Suspended ceilings with recessed lighting troffers define the library module.

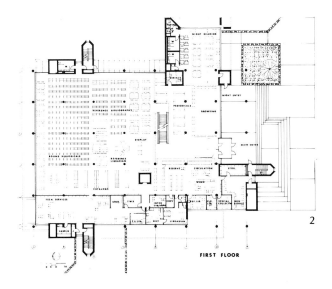

FIRST FLOOR 2

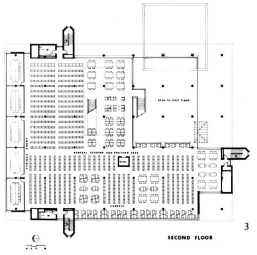

SECOND FLOOR 3

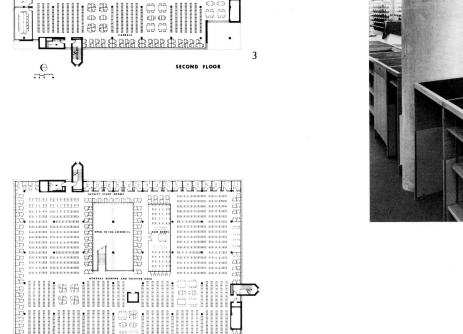

THIRD FLOOR 4

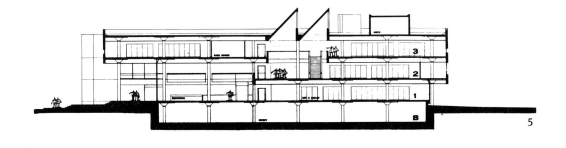

5

6

1 principal elevation and entrance
2 groundfloor plan
3 second-floor plan
4 third-floor plan
5 longitudinal section
6 interior

1

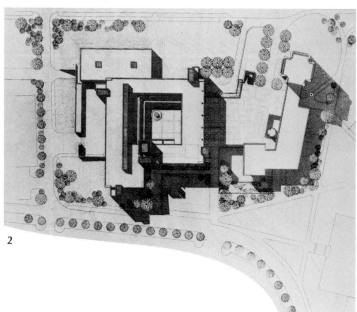

2

Physics Building, Princeton University, 1963

Planning and design of the Jadwin Physical Laboratory demanded close coordination with an adjacent mathematics building being planned to the north of the complex. Although both architects worked out the individual building solutions independently, agreement was reached at an early stage on the vocabulary of materials to integrate the two buildings with each other and with the rest of the campus. The materials agreed upon were brick, granite, and glass framed in anodized aluminum. The buildings are linked by a plaza, which is actually the roof of the jointly used math/physics library. Located at the east end of the College Walk, a prime pedestrian circulation route connecting the academic area with the stadium, the new plaza has become a way station, enhancing rather than cutting off or disrupting this traditional pathway.

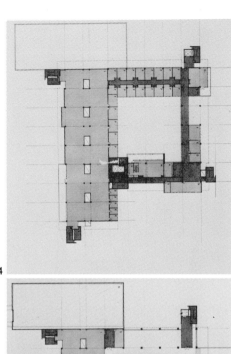

4

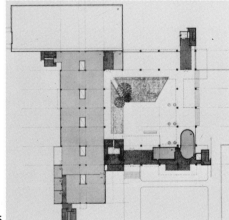

5

3

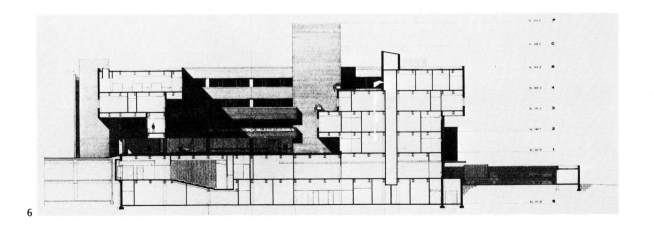

1 main facade from plaza
2 site plan
3 overall view, model
4 groundfloor plan
5 second-floor plan
6 section

6

7

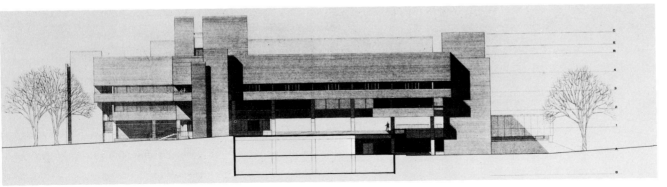

8

7 entrance detail
8 plaza elevation
9 service side
10 entrance courtyard
11 cyclotron

126

9

10

The plan form emerged from the concept of wrapping the theoreticians' (think) offices around an open court and placing the experimentalists' (do) laboratories in a flexible laboratory research block. Corridors ringing the building are enlivened and humanized by frequent alcoves equipped with seating and chalkboards to encourage communication between faculty and researchers from both parts of the building. With views out of the building or down into the courtyard, these corridor alcoves also provide a means of orientation and relationship with the world outside.

11

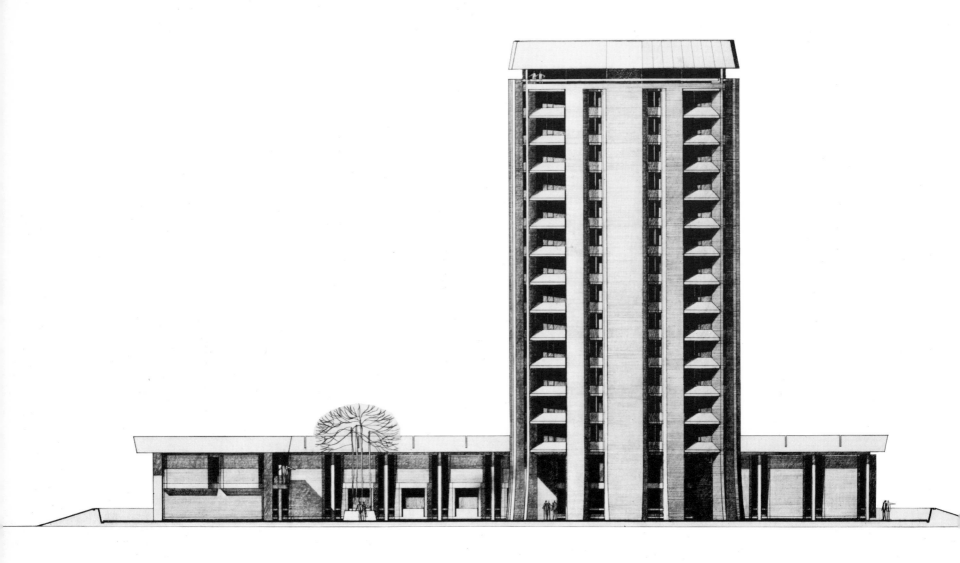

1 elevation
2 typical tower plan
3 dining and lounge building

2

128

3

Bowdoin Senior Center, 1961

Inspired by the well-tried traditions of Oxford and Cambridge, Bowdoin College in Brunswick, Maine, decided to give its 200 seniors their own environment—somewhat secluded from the rest of the campus—where they could live, study, and dine in close contact with faculty members and distinguished guests. The Bowdoin Senior Center thus contains three separate buildings accommodating three distinct functions: a residential tower, a residence and apartments for the director and visiting professors, and a main dining commons with lounges and seminar rooms. Although dominant in a small, closely knit, classical campus, the tower symbolizes this new educational endeavor—standing a little apart from yet looking out over the rest of the complex. The three buildings are unified by brick and concrete construction, bold limestone cornices, and the clearly defined, bermed terrace or podium on which they all sit.

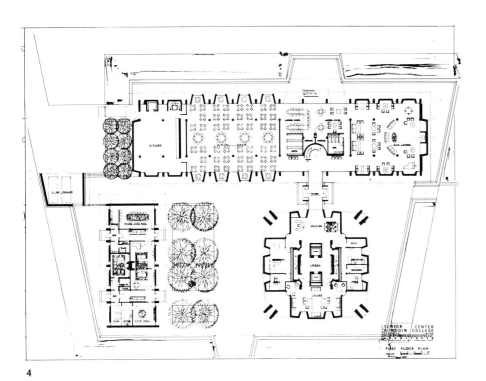

4

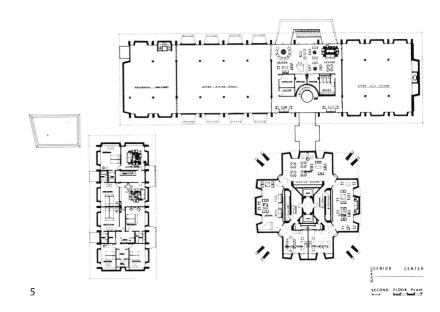

5

SENIOR CENTER

SECOND FLOOR PLAN

The 16-story tower is in sympathy with the tall pine trees that characterize the site. In both tower and low-rise buildings, projecting brick bays are employed to express the study or seating alcoves within. In addition to student suites and resident faculty living quarters, the tower also contains seminar and conference rooms, a small library, visitors' lounges, and the center's administrative offices. A common foyer links the tower with the commons building. The director's residence is separated by a paved and landscaped court.

The number of students and faculty to be accommodated on a restricted site dictated a high-rise solution. On a typical floor the symmetrical tower consists of four groups of individual study bedrooms arranged in suites of four—two on either side of a corner living room. Bathrooms interconnect the suites. The main dining room and lounge on the ground floor of the low-rise building have the advantage of double-story ceiling height. Two smaller lounges form a bridge over the central section between these two spaces.

Self-contained, but in contact with the rest of the campus and the world outside, the Senior Center provides students with the opportunity to develop their own resources as a transition between college and their careers. The buildings are intended to express and reinforce these endeavors.

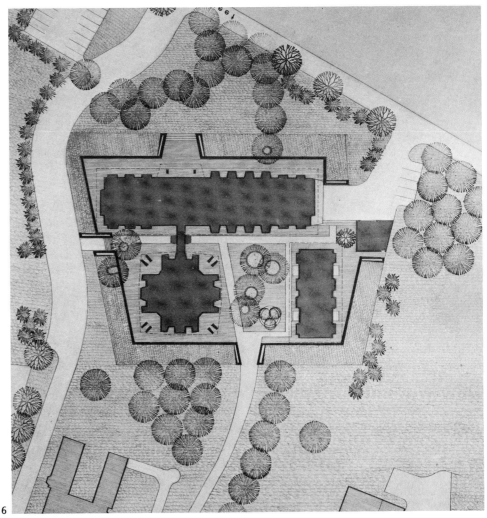

6

7

8

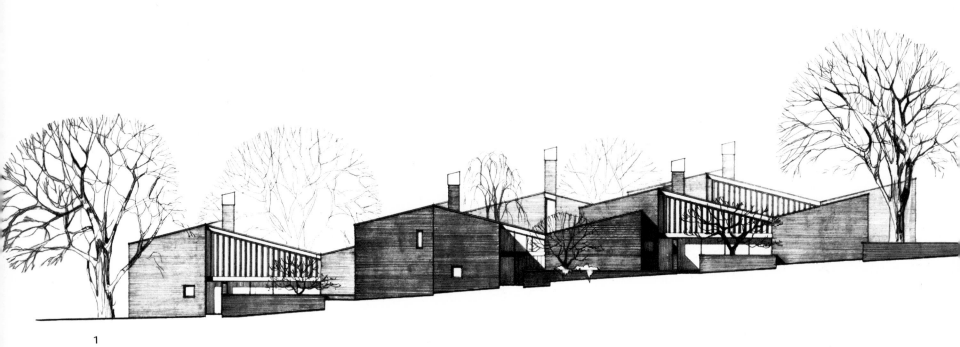

1

1 elevations
2 general view and central courtyard
3 site plan
4 floor plans

Dana Hall Schools, Wellesley, Massachusetts, 1962

The first replacement for some of its older houses, this residential complex for the Dana Hall Schools was designed and detailed with meticulous care to maintain the domestic scale and palette of materials of existing buildings in a fine residential neighborhood. The split-level solution allows the buildings, interconnected by a subterranean passage, to step gently down the sloping site. Although arranged in a relatively tight cluster, the houses are oriented out toward the rest of the campus, the entry courts and larger common courtyards providing sheltered and intimate outdoor counterparts to the interior space. The courts, steps, and walkways paved in concrete and the brick walls and copper shed roofs emphasize the village-like character of the complex. Each house accommodates 32 girls in single and double rooms and also includes a student lounge, laundry, and a faculty suite.

2

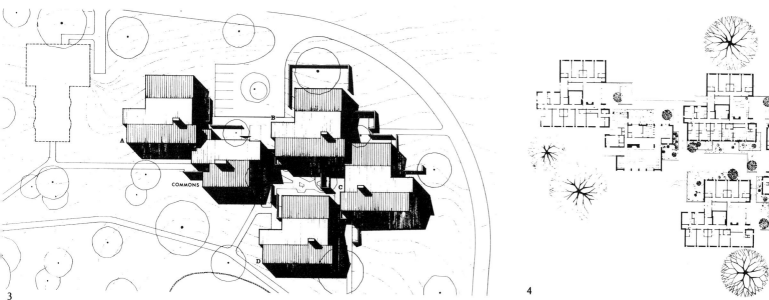

3

4

5   entrance view
6   general view
7   pedestrian street

With a seating capacity of 600, the dining commons is by far the largest building on the campus. But sensitive use of the hilly site and a compatible roof formation made it possible to maintain the domestic scale of the rest of the campus. The two-level building has special meeting areas and student lounges below the main dining facility. The lounges have become a popular gathering place for students and are in use most of the day. The dining area has the benefit of expansive views out over a beautiful campus. The slope of the site allows the kitchen on the second level and a service entrance at grade. Materials are brick with precast concrete trim.

1 main-floor plan
2 lower-level entrance plan
3 general view

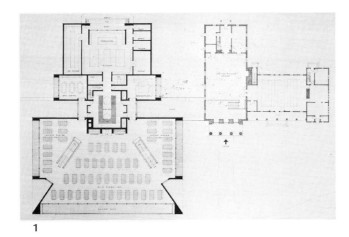

1

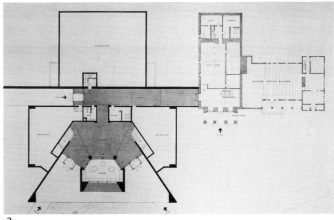

2

3

1

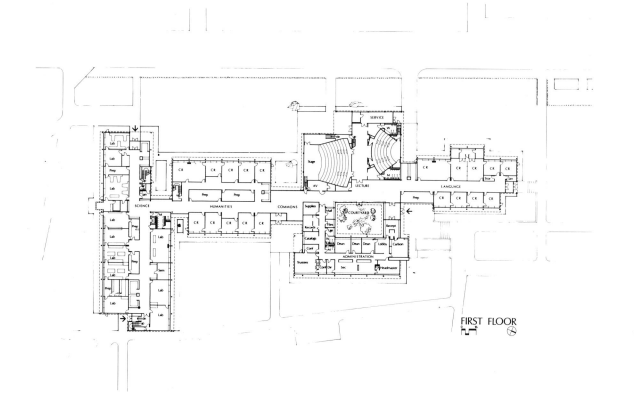

FIRST FLOOR

1 gable ends
2 student entrance
3 science wing
4 auditorium entrance

Tabor Academy, Marion, Massachusetts, 1969

These buildings evolved from a master plan, phased to replace the entire academic facility of a boy's private school and take it into the future. Because the school is in a small coastal town with a fine heritage of New England regional clapboard and shingle architecture, the building is broken down into pavilions to be more compatible with the scale of their environs. Shed roofs and shingle walls reinforce their unity with their antecedents.

The central administration, two lecture halls, and language, mathematics, and science facilities are ranged along both sides of a broad, central spine. Passing through courtyards, windowed corners giving carefully controlled views of the outdoors, this spine or central corridor is a cheerful place, the hub of the life of the school.

The structure—expressed in the building's exterior—is reinforced concrete for permanence and low maintenance combined with cedar shingle walls weathering to a silver gray in the salt air. Traditional wood trim is painted white in harmony with the indigenous architecture.

137

1

University of California at Santa Cruz—College # 5, 1967

The college is conceived as a compact quadrangle recalling aspects of Christ Church College, Oxford, and a small town in the Maritime Alps.

The desire for compactness—without resorting to elevator high-rise buildings—stems from the university's prescription to leave areas between colleges as undisturbed landscape. The forest, the deep draws, the pastoral slopes, and the sea are an inescapable part of the intercollege scene. The student, as he goes from college to college or from college to center, is constantly aware of this compelling landscape.

A purposeful attempt is made in this college to give it a sense of identity—a sense of place—and to give a different and more cultivated "environment" within the walls as compared with that on the outside.

A college—like a town—has its place of work, its residential quarters, its marketplace, and its place of public assembly and seat of government. The houses grouped around a two-level court, form the walls that enclose the "town square" and separate it from the natural landscape. The houses are mostly four stories high—one is five, owing to a change in grade. They in turn are divided into living–study suites of various sizes. Apartments for faculty are near the major entrances.

The academic areas—class and seminar rooms—are placed on the ground floor of some of the houses to encourage a mixture of student activities and to get multiuse (perhaps at night) from some of the academic spaces.

Beyond the residential court, to carry the town analogy further, is the public square, the seat of government and the place for public assembly. Here are the administrative offices, faculty studies, tutorial offices, and classrooms in a two-story building surrounding a small fountain courtyard. Here also are the dining hall and student commons.

The views from this group of buildings are controlled. From the courtyard all distant vistas are framed by buildings or buildings and trees, so that only glimpses are obtained. The main view of the sea is from the dining hall.

The 800 student population includes approximately 250 commuters, who are by design integrated into the college. To reach classrooms or locker facilities, they enter the residential court from the north and become immediately involved in this center of activity or continue to the administrative court and dining commons.

2

3

1 rendered site plan by Hugh Stubbins
2 view from the south
3 academic court
4 residential court
5 environment

4

The college is coeducational with emphasis on the performing arts. The Performing Arts Building, not part of the satellite college, is located within easy walking distance. There are also opportunities for student performances and exhibitions within the court areas beneath the redwoods. The structural frame is concrete with exterior walls of stucco on steel studs. Mission tile is used for roofing. Interior finishes include exposed concrete, painted gypsum board, and redwood.

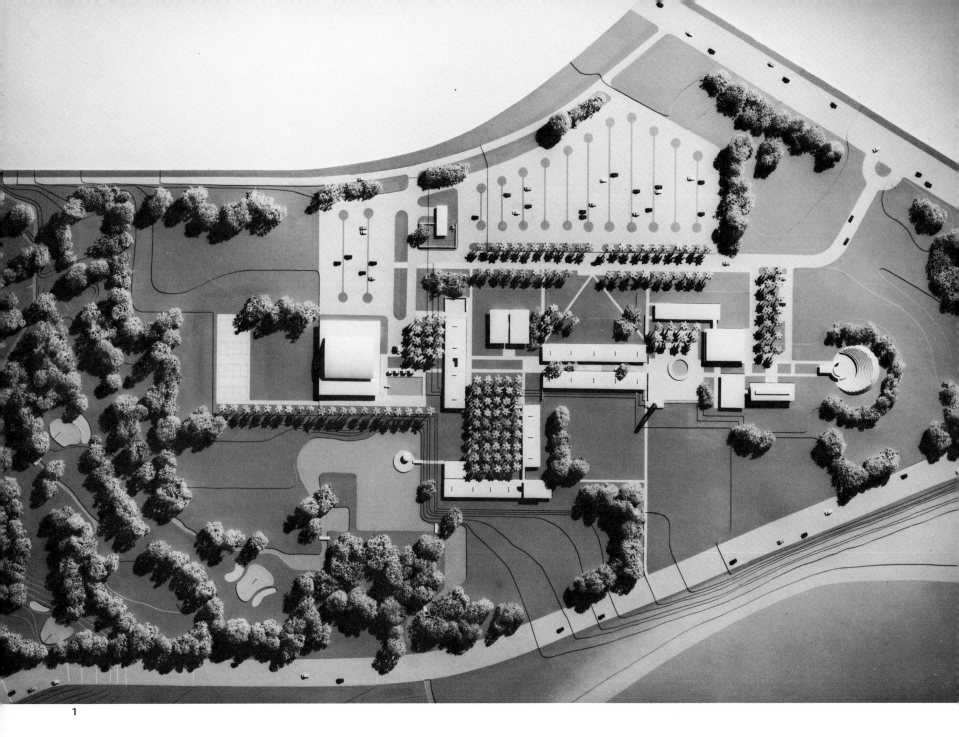

1

1 site plan, model
2 aerial view, model
3 architectural details

Gulf Coast Community College, 1958

An essentially linear configuration for this master plan allows maximum exposure of the buildings to the bay. It also creates a sequence of carefully planned outdoor spaces to complement the architecture and provide interesting views within the campus and from the highways bordering the site. Because parking and vehicular circulation are kept to the periphery, the campus itself becomes a pedestrian domain.

The driveway terminates at the administration building. As one walks through the campus, one passes through a courtyard flanked by the auditorium—planned for public as well as campus use—and the arts and crafts building. The student street—lined with classrooms—leads through to another square or courtyard with the library to one side and, through a grove of palm trees, the science building. Terminating the long visual access is the student commons with dining facilities and social rooms. Beyond this are the athletic building and playing fields, which have their own direct vehicular access. Since this campus was designed for commuting students, the parking is stretched along one side with multiple access points to the buildings.

A common structural system for all the buildings was developed to bring unity to the entire complex. The structure consists of concrete floors on grade and reinforced masonry columns and masonry walls supporting short-span concrete lintels. These, in turn, support a roof structure of full-span, precast double-Ts placed side by side. The double-Ts project beyond walls and lintels to create a generous and protective overhang shading walks and classrooms from the hot sun. The structure was designed so that all elements could be manufactured within a few miles of the site.

2

3

1

1 portal and ramp
2 groundfloor plan
3 lower-level plan
4 second-floor plan

The Rochester Institute of Technology, 1962

The new RIT campus was planned at one time by five architectural firms, who, on this occasion, managed to collaborate in sufficient depth to produce a very homogeneous environment. Our firm was responsible for the College of Fine and Applied Arts, the College of Graphic Arts and Photography—a very large academic building with an unusually diverse program. The activities housed in this building include printing in all its forms, photography, painting, sculpture, illustration, textiles, woodworking, silversmithing, and so forth. Each department has its own space and support facilities, although there are two major shared areas—the skylit exhibition room and the large lecture hall.

Since the building occupies a key position in the academic core, the organization of its elements, circulation, and massing derive from its role as an "anchor building." The five-story, L-shaped structure defines a spacious courtyard—the central academic quadrangle—as well as a portal to the center of the campus. A broad pedestrian path—running through the building—allows students using the main commuter parking convenient access to this and other campus buildings. Exhibition space opening onto this walkway provides an opportunity for students to display their work and their activities for those passing through.

Whereas the colleges are interconnected to form a continuous structure, they maintain a clearly defined individual identity with separate entrances. Exterior terraces—a device for scaling down the apparent volume of the building in relation to the courtyard—also reinforce this identity.

Organized around a system of large—34-foot-square—structural bays, the building has considerable functional flexibility. The structure is a poured-in-place concrete frame with brick cavity walls. The ironspot brick used on the exterior walls is the major unifying material selected by the collaborating firms to establish a consistent design vocabulary.

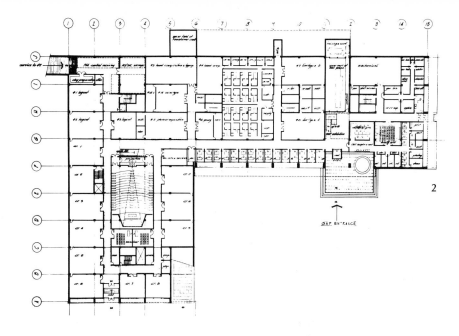

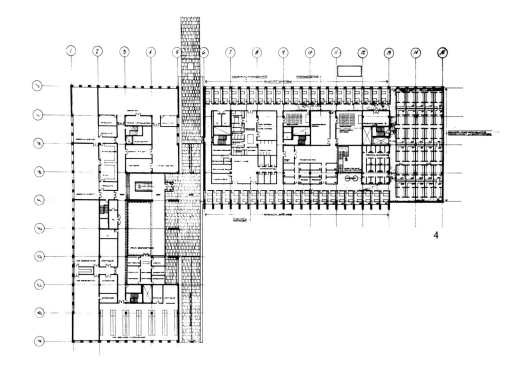

5

6

7

8

146

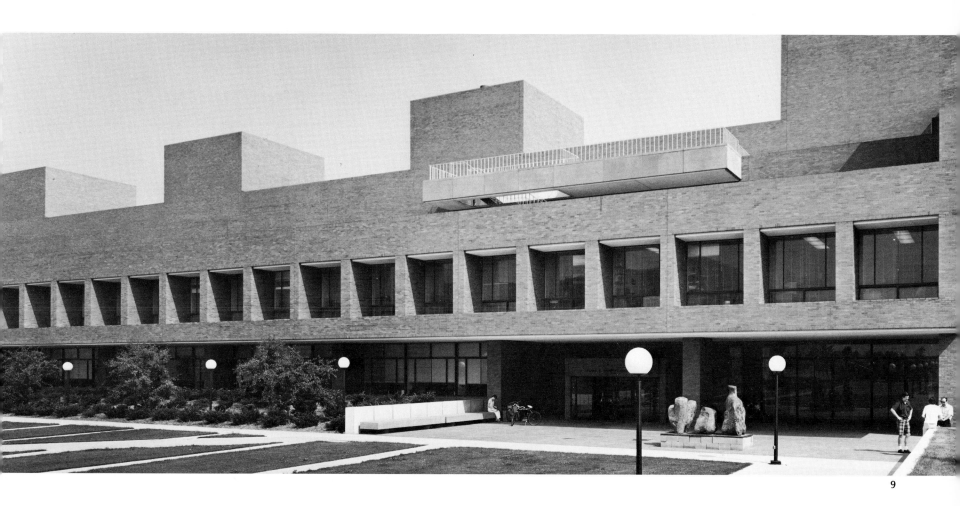

9

1

National Technical Institute for the Deaf
Rochester, New York, 1967

The isolation of the deaf behind a barrier of silence not only
deprives them of their human rights by limiting their potential
for independent and productive lives but also deprives the
professions and industry of a valuable resource of talent. The
National Technical Institute for the Deaf (NTID) is dedicated
and designed to provide an annual enrollment of some 750
students with the opportunity to pursue postsecondary
technical education leading to active participation in the
world of work and to gain this in close communication with
the hearing student population of the Rochester Institute of
Technology (RIT). Funded by the Department of Health,
Education, and Welfare—under President Johnson—and
sponsored by RIT, the institute will also operate as a training
center to assist in the preparation of qualified professionals to
instruct and serve the deaf.

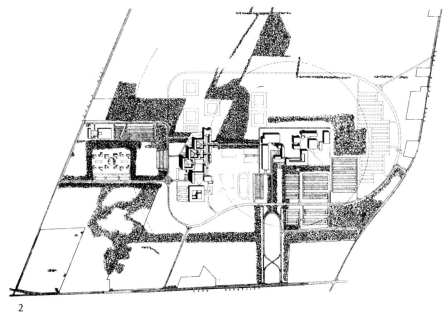

2

Because our firm had already designed the Arts complex for the RIT campus, we were familiar with the site and environmental requirements for additions. In approaching the design of the NTID complex, there were three major concerns:

- To provide close integration and communion with the RIT campus in buildings that would express the identity of the NTID students, their pride in themselves, and their confidence in their future.
- To incorporate the sophisticated technology required for the education of the deaf.
- To use light, color, texture, and space to heighten the educational use and enjoyment of those perceptions in which the deaf have no handicap.

The new complex consists of three types of facility expressed in separate buildings: the academic center, the dining commons, and student housing. Although each building is clearly defined, integration with each other and existing RIT housing at the southern end of the site is achieved by means of landscaped courts and below-grade circulation. The relationship of the new buildings to the existing campus is further reinforced by compatibility of scale, fenestration, and the use of the same warm-toned brick for exterior walls. Bridging the access street to the residential buildings, the dining commons forms a dramatic gateway linking RIT and NTID and marking the introduction of a new presence in the campus environment.

The academic building is a 300-foot-square brick structure organized on three levels around a two-story, skylit pedestrian mall that runs north-south through the building, giving staff and students the opportunity to glimpse the full range of activities as they pass along. Located at the center of the building, groups of four fan-shaped, multipurpose lecture halls are planned around shared media centers from which audiovisual material can be preprogrammed, controlled, and directed to any one or all four of the halls. Tiered swivel seating ensures uninterrupted sight lines between lecturer and student—of paramount importance for students whose visual perception is their chief means of communication.

1 aerial view
2 campus plan
3 second-floor plan
4 groundfloor plan
5 section

149

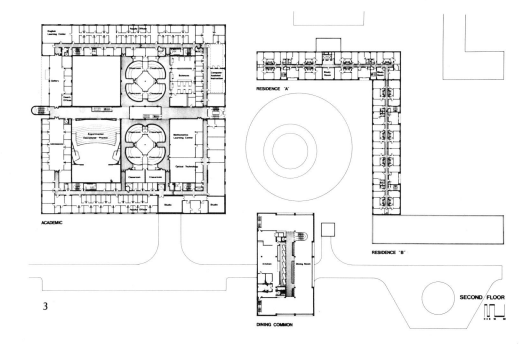

3

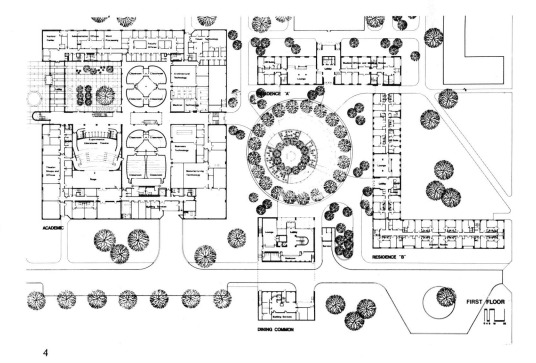

4

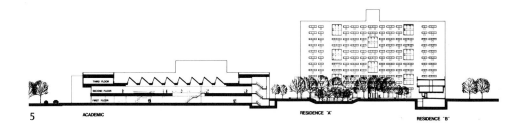

5

6 entrance detail
7 courtyard
8 lecture room
9 high-rise residence

6

7

8

150

Since NTID will sponsor and produce its own television programs, a fully equipped television center with two studios is part of the academic center. There are special anechoic testing rooms for audiological evaluation. Extensive provision has been made for computer-assisted instruction—representing a union of visual media, programmed instruction, and computer science. Throughout the complex, a combination of strobe and colored lighting is used as an effective means of emergency/call communication. A very high level of acoustic performance has been achieved to ensure proper functioning of electronic hearing aids and sensitive equipment required for audiological testing and evaluation.

9

Special Problems

Although every job is, in an important sense, a special problem, some are complicated by the demand for highly specialized facilities, a high degree of technical complexity, a difficult site, or a particularly low budget. To reach appropriate solutions in these cases requires teamwork that is more open and creative than is usual. The architect may not always be the guiding creative force, sometimes the real design innovation may come from the consulting engineers.

In the effort to answer specialized problems there is sometimes a danger of a certain lack of balance in the solution. In trying, for example, to provide a fully flexible stage and an acoustically perfect auditorium, we may be tempted to neglect the unity of the total building form or the comfort of the backstage personnel. The unity of a building within itself and with its surroundings thus becomes a matter of conscious concern. Expression of its prime function— though necessary and legitimate—cannot be allowed to strike a discordant note in the wider environment of the street and its neighborhood. It is as important to solve these problems as it is to solve the special central program requirements.

For this reason I have never found it possible to adopt any universal building genre or design theme that makes its appearance again and again on different sites and for different clients with different programs. I have felt bound to subject each solution to the rigorous discipline of logic and to remember that—however pressing the individual program needs—the designer is working within the framework of a considerable lifespan for his building, which may involve radical changes of function.

I believe this tendency to look for a universal theme springs from a yearning for the security of an accepted tradition of problem solving in an age of global disturbance and deep personal malaise. But we are living and working in a profession in which the disciplines imposed by traditional philosophies and limited technology have given way to whatever discipline the artist is willing to impose upon himself. Our great obligation is to respond responsibly to the opportunities, dangers, and challenges that this freedom holds. In such a context, solutions must be sought painstakingly and individually—by balancing the pressing needs of a particular client against the equally insistent, if less easily determined demands of future generations and a wider environment.

1

1 general view
2 plan—proscenium configuration
3 plan—Elizabethan configuration
4 plan—theater in the round configuration

5 ceiling raft
6 Elizabethan form
7 lobby terrace
8 section

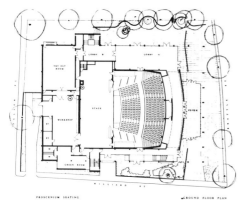

2

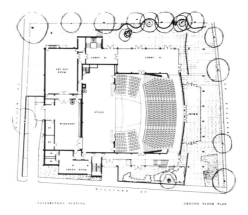

3

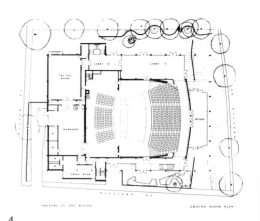

4

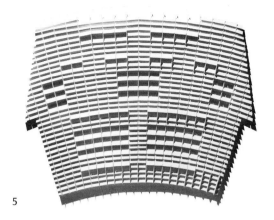

5

6

7

Loeb Drama Center, Cambridge, 1958

Harvard's directive that the Loeb Drama Center be designed "for the production of plays for audiences rather than for the teaching of dramatic arts and skills; that the stage be adaptable enough to enable classical or modern plays to be presented in a manner consistent with the style in which they are written; and that this be accomplished without sacrificing the view from a single seat" led to the design of the first fully flexible theater in the United States. In collaboration with a distinguished team of playwrights, actors, and electronics and acoustical experts, we devised a solution that manipulates seating and stage from proscenium configuration, to Elizabethan thrust stage, to theater in-the-round. This was achieved by putting the seating closest to the stage (about one-third of the total) on nine elevators so that all can be moved within a time frame of less than an hour. The first 140 seats are on motorized platforms and can be shifted to the right and left sides. The stage—also on lifts—can be converted into a variety of configurations.

Since the building is in a predominantly traditional, residential area, we kept the design as unobtrusive as possible, retained the trees, and used the second-level offices and rehearsal rooms encircling the stage to form a two-story volume to minimize the projecting form of stage house and fly gallery.

Archibald MacLeish and the theater director Robert Chapman, who wrote the program, expressed most eloquently the ambience the building was designed to fulfill: "It should be a building which, as building, will create the sense of excitement and expectation which most American theatres so flatly fail to give . . . but though the theatre must be beautiful, its builders must also remember that 'the play's the thing.' The building should not be so architecturally exciting and excited that plays produced in it will be overshadowed by their frame."

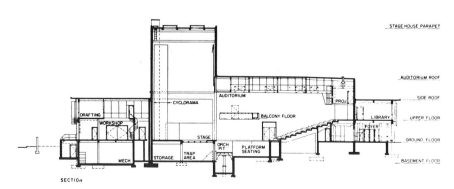

8

Veterans Stadium, Philadelphia, 1966

The chief problem in a multipurpose stadium is that desirable seating positions for football and baseball are quite different and mutually opposed. Football fans all want to sit on the 50 yard line, but the coveted baseball positions are along the foul lines or behind home plate. Moreover, circular schemes put many of the most desirable seats too far from the action; a square or other polygon, while putting fans closer to the action, creates "angle of view" difficulties. To find a better remedy for this dilemma we devised a new form for the 50,000- to 65,000-seat Philadelphia Stadium: a slightly arced square based on eight points of radii of two concentric circles that I have called an "Octorad."

A major consideration was the city's mandate that the stadium seat no fewer than 65,000 for football and no more than 50,000 for baseball. This meant that, during the baseball season, 15,000 seats had to "disappear." This was achieved by rolling away 8000 seats from the football configuration, to enlarge the playing surface for the baseball outfield, and by partially screening the remainder behind two large computerized outfield scoreboards, which are hydraulically lowered into the stands for football.

Pedestrian and auto ramps connect surrounding parking lots and Pattison Avenue with the 30-foot-wide podium surrounding the stadium at the third level, which in turn leads into the main concourse. At this concourse, ramps, escalators, and elevators convey people up or down to their seats, which are organized in four bold color zones for ease of orientation. Clubhouse, locker and meeting rooms, the main receiving dock, and service facilities are on the first level, below grade. Press and television facilities, private boxes, and a club restaurant are located in the lower edge of the second tier of seats.

Structure of the stadium is a combination of cast-in-place and precast concrete with precast seat step units.

2

3

1 overall view, model (baseball configuration)
2 people
3 "octorad" geometry

1

157

Berlin Congress Hall, 1955

When it was built in 1956–1957, the Berlin Congress Hall represented a new building type. At the time of its completion, the UN General Assembly in New York, the UNESCO Building in Paris, and the Conference Hall in Caracas were the only structures in the world with comparable facilities. The aim of all those concerned with the building of the *Kongresshalle* was to enrich the cultural life of the city by making it a meetingplace for the scholars of all nations.

The spirit in which the *Kongresshalle* was conceived is expressed in these words of Benjamin Franklin carved into the stone walls of the building "God grant that not only love of liberty, but a thorough knowledge of the rights of man may pervade all the nations of the earth, so that a philospher may set his foot anywhere on its surface and say, 'this is my country.'"

The building consists of two elements integrated into a single expression of the theme. The main auditorium—the meeting hall for international discussions—strikes the dominant note in the composition. Rising 60 feet above a raised plaza, it states unmistakably the primary purpose of the building. Surrounding it on lower levels are the spaces provided for activities essential to and contributory to its functions.

1

The site for the building—a level, 11-acre plot near the center
of the city, bounded by the Tiergarten and the River Spree, is
at the heart of Berlin, politically and historically—as well as
geographically. The Tiergarten area has been the seat of past
German governments and is the location for many
commemorative monuments. The building is at the focal point
of cultural life—within the western part of the city, yet directly
accessible and easily visible from East Berlin. It has become an
important orienting feature from the air, the distinctive shape
of the auditorium roof, imposed on the rectangle of the plaza,
being an easily recognizable landmark.

The roof itself is hung between two arches and a compression
ring surrounding the auditorium. It touches the deck lightly at ·
two points, and two large buttresses rising from the ground
support the ends of the two converging arches, which rise
wide and high to shelter the hall, as well as the large area
around it.

The roof is equally important in its symbolic value as an
expression of the spirit in which the building was conceived.
At the time, daring—and with the grace of great strength—it
appears completely free. From the midpoint of the arches,
where it dips lowest, it opens wide in two directions, inviting
and giving light.

1 concept drawing
2 construction, aerial view
3 section
4 groundfloor plan
5 plan of hall and terrace
6 lobby near bar
7 the hall
8 stairway to hall

2

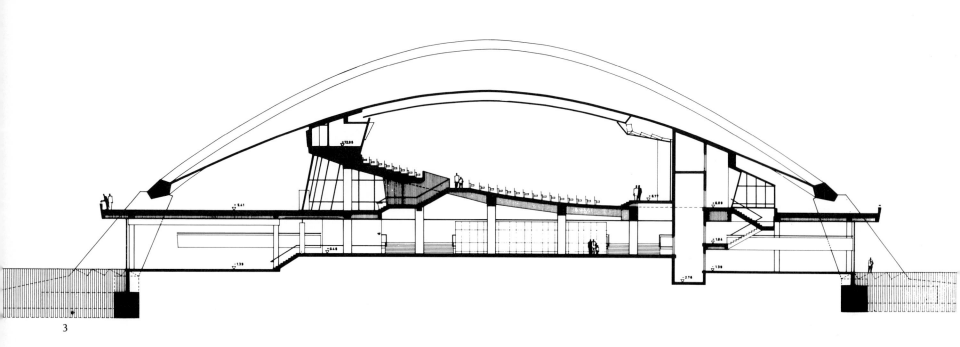

3

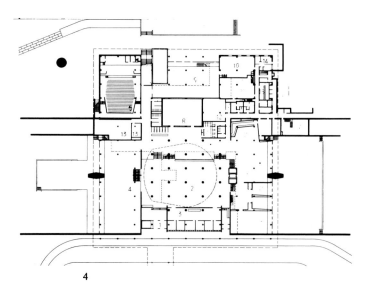

4

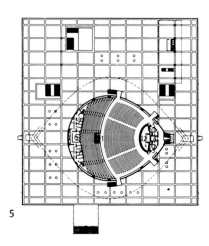

5

162

To accentuate the supremacy of the main hall, the site was given a gentle upward slope around the building, but the lower floor still remains at the existing natural level of the Tiergarten. The area for ancillary facilities was thus keyed down to a truly fundamental position, that of supporting the auditorium but never presuming to equal it. Catching the rise of surrounding earth, the main hall continues the upward sweeping lines to become the pinnacle, not of the building alone, but of the very land itself.

In its space between the street and the river, the building reaches out to those who approach either by land or water. From the street it is accessible to motorists via drives leading beneath the overhang of the upper plaza to the main entrance on the ground floor and to pedestrians by a broad walkway bridging the reflecting pool. On the river side, a boat landing and broad stairs to terraced levels admit water travelers. Parking is provided at the east side, where space is available and where it is sufficiently distant not to disturb the unity of the structure or to hamper pedestrian traffic. Entrances to all levels connect the parking ramp with the building. On the west side, a landscaped park, set with trees, walks, and sitting places, slopes gently upward from the river and provides easy access to all parts of the hall.

The deck from which the auditorium rises is actually a terrace–plaza overlooking the river and park, providing a place for promenading and for a terrace cafe in the shadow of the arches. Viewed from the west, this terrace–plaza appears just above ground level. The slight upward slope of the site on all sides appears to be followed through by the increased upward thrust of the arches.

Inside, offices for the use of conference personnel open off the great central lobby on the ground floor. A two-level lounge and snack bar near the small conference rooms is designed and furnished for informal meetings. On the west side, a large exhibition hall opens into a lower garden. There are also committee rooms affording conference space for groups of 25 to 100 people. Some of these rooms open into a walled garden.

Stairs from the ground floor rise to the upper lobby, giving access to the main auditorium and the plaza. Here, in the great conference hall in which the entire project culminates, 1200 people may sit together, speak, and be understood by means of multilingual translation facilities.

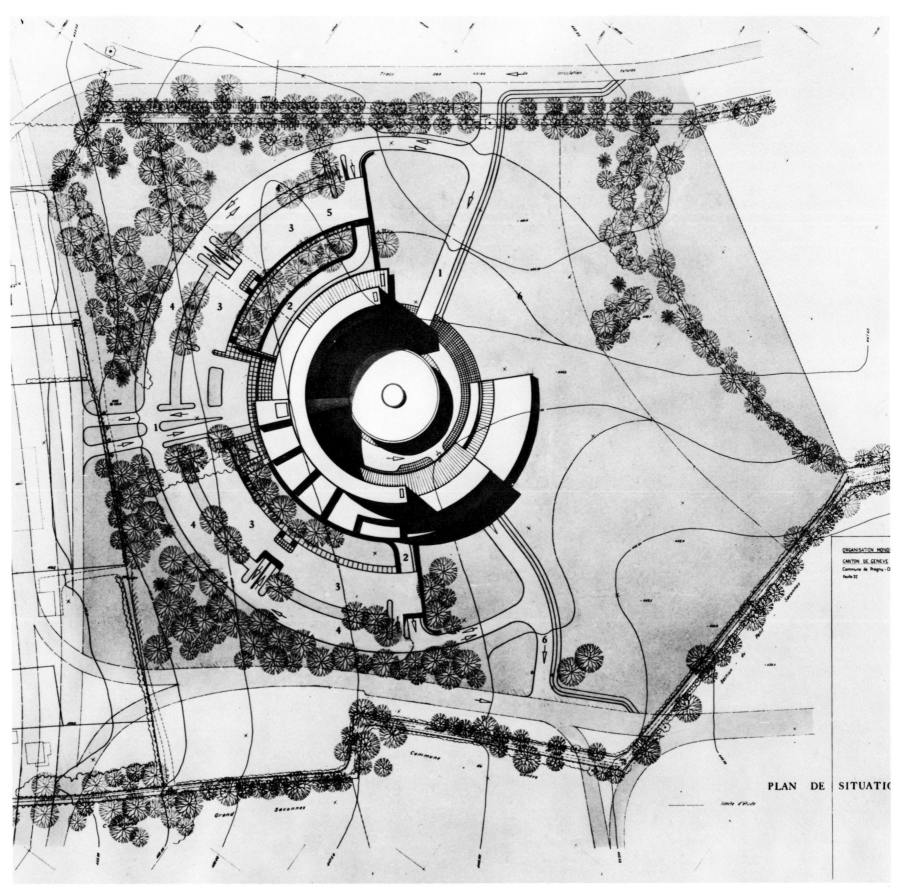

PLAN DE SITUATION

1 rendered site plan
2 approach view
3 aerial view

1

164

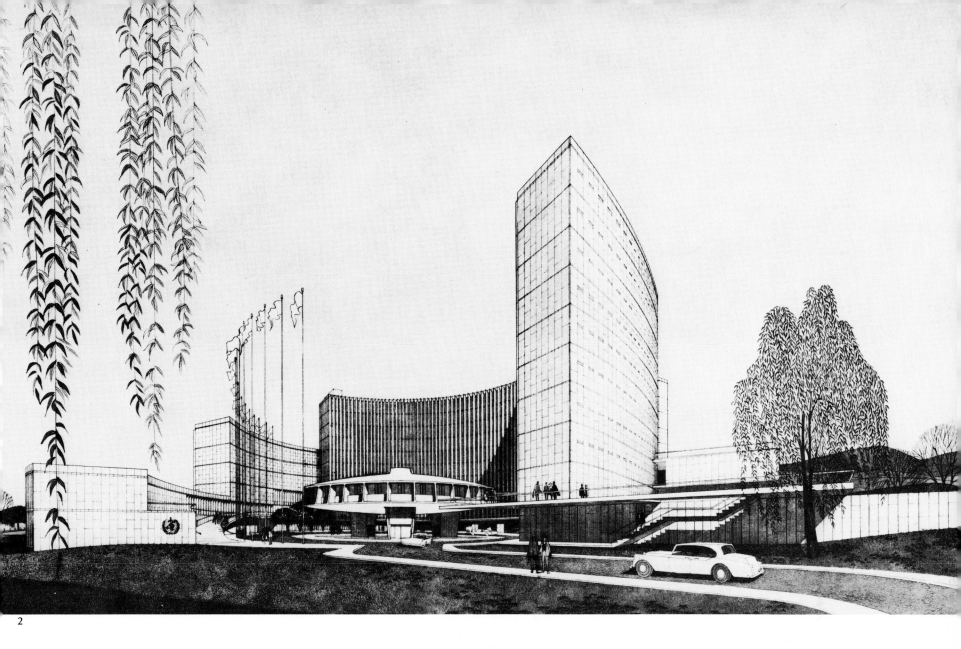

2

World Health Organization Project, 1960

In 1960 an international competition was held for the design of the World Health Organization's headquarters in Geneva. Architects from member nations were invited to compete, and we and Eero Saarinen were the two United States architectural firms selected for the competition, which neither of us won.

Our scheme—for a gently sloping site overlooking Lake Geneva—was based on a series of concentric circles focusing on the round congress hall in the center. The slender, curved office building looks out over the lake, while conference rooms at the perimeter—stepping down one per floor—are oriented in the opposite direction. The two-level parking garage repeats the curved theme. The main approach to the complex culminates in a circular driveway of impressive proportions.

3

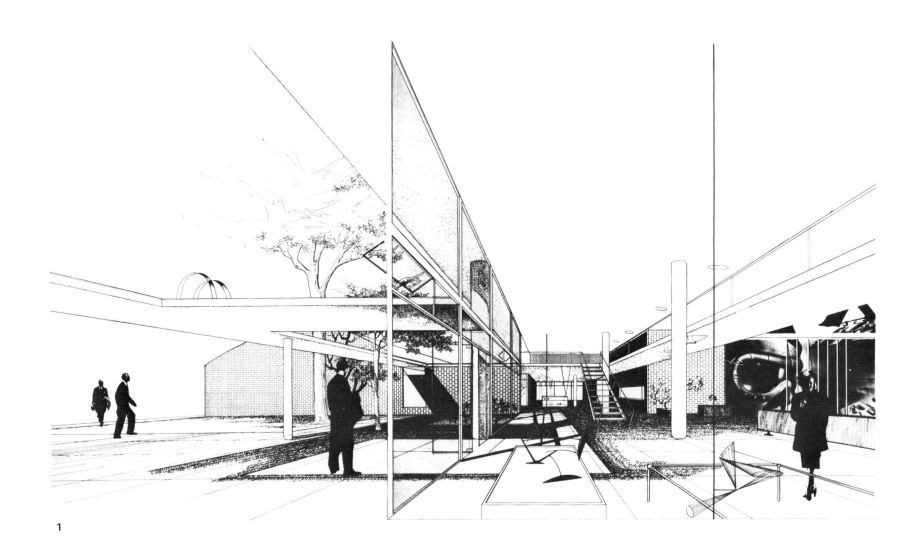

1 inside-outside view of lobby
2 aerial view of office building and plant
3 location and site plan

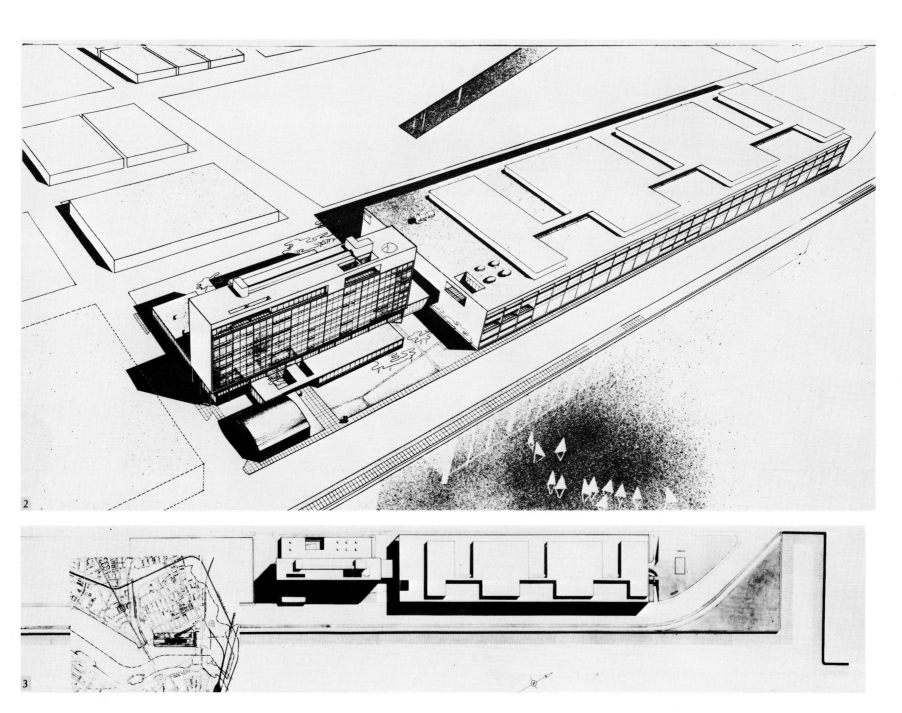

Polaroid Plant Project, Cambridge, 1945

Research, administrative, and manufacturing space are accommodated in a series of flexible structures designed for ease of maintenance, low running costs, and possible future conversion to a different use. A service and circulation spine is closed off from the manufacturing space by a series of airlocks to keep out dust and other airborne impurities.
Manufacturing areas are completely air conditioned, the main equipment on the roof and major ducts running over the service backbone.

Administrative functions are housed in a separate but connected structure, with a six-story research building above. On a prominent site overlooking a wide river, the complex, never built, includes landscaped walks and courtyards and makes generous use of glass walls to take advantage of views and create a pleasant flow of indoor–outdoor space.

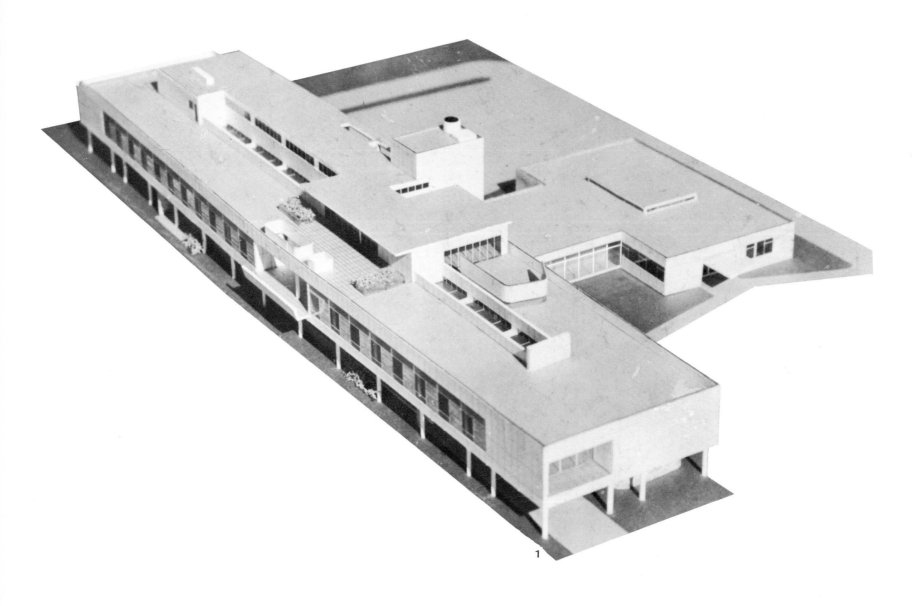

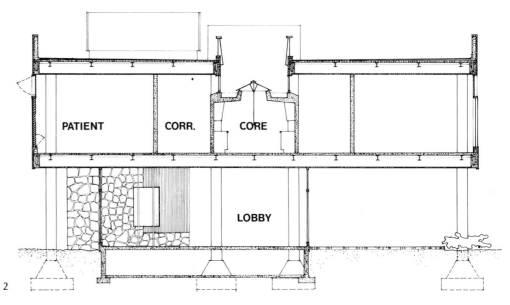

1 overall view, model
2 section
3 third floor, operating suite
4 second floor, patient care
5 groundfloor, administration, services
  and outpatient

PATIENT

CORR.

CORE

LOBBY

168

OPERAT'G FLOOR

3

NURSING FLOOR

4

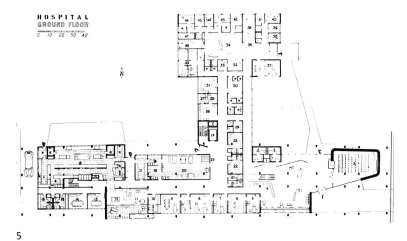

HOSPITAL
GROUND FLOOR
0 10 20 30 40

5

U.S. Gypsum Hospital Project, Chicago, 1944

Designed for the U.S. Gypsum Company as part of an advertising campaign to establish better standards for postwar buildings, this hospital project is probably the first published example of the double-loaded corridor plan. Designed to serve a community of about 30,000 people, the hospital program required maximum interior flexibility to permit easy adaptation to changing needs and developing medical technology.

The solution places all entrances, services, and clinical facilities at ground level for ease of access and a clear relationship with other elements of the plan. Boiler plant, storage, and morgue are in the basement. The second level, or nursing floor consists of a series of patient rooms surrounding a service core. Each single bedroom is designed on a module to make it readily convertible to a double room. Bed capacity can be increased from 60 to 85 without overcrowding. By making alternate partitions demountable and soundproof, the plan permits easy adaptation to ward space if required. The operating suite is on the top floor, and radiography is in the link connecting the hospital with the out-patient center.

Saint Peter's Church, New York, 1972

St. Peter's Lutheran Church is the first major urban church to be built in midtown Manhattan for many years. Its location within The Citicorp complex makes it doubly unique. Replacing, on almost exactly the same site, a turn-of-the-century Gothic church—demolished when the site was cleared—the new St. Peter's continues a fine tradition of worship and public service in the modern city.

Its relationship with past and future, its location at a busy street intersection and subway interchange, and its concern to bridge the gap between the world of work and the life of the spirit have led the church congregation to characterize their new venture "life at the intersection."

St. Peter's sold its property and sanctioned demolition of the original church in return for condominium ownership of more than 45,000 square feet of new church space on the same corner of the site. Contractual arrangements with Citicorp gave the church the assurance of a substantially free-standing building with "nothing but sky overhead." Proceeds from the transaction have enabled the church to finance a much larger new building and fund its forthcoming programs.

St. Peter's has been an involved and democratic client. A socially and community-oriented group, it provides numerous community services, some available on a 24-hour basis. The church council elected a building committee to act on its behalf in the planning and construction of the new building and a design task force to represent the council in working directly with the architects to develop the design of the new church. A great number of design forums and hearings have been held throughout the design process to communicate ideas and progress to the congregation.

A diverse group of people, united in their commitment to the symbolic, spiritual, practical, and aesthetic values of the new building, have been an intimate part of the evolution of the new church. If the congregation has not exactly designed its own church, it has put its insights, feelings, hopes, and fears into the design process, and this must be the lifeblood of good architecture. St. Peter's Church is thus, not an empty monument to the virtuosity of its architect, but a vibrant expression of the community that helped in every step of its development. This community involvement, much talked about but seldom practiced, has been an exciting, often difficult, but ultimately rewarding experience.

The physical relationship of the church to the office building complex was one of the major areas of discussion in initial planning sessions. Should the church be closely integrated with the secular buildings or should it be completely detached? A sculpture in a garden? Although the sculptural theme was attractive, the church did not want to be thought of as "a piece of artwork in the bank's front yard." It wanted its own strong identity and a clear statement of its presence on Lexington Avenue.

1

2

1 general view, model
2 view from Lexington Avenue
3 street-level plan
4 plaza
5 section
6 sanctuary

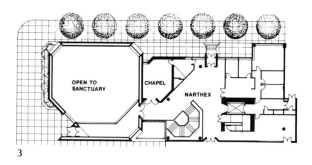

3

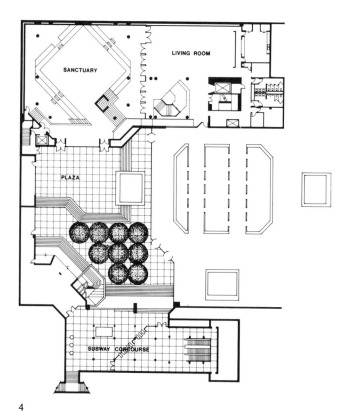

4

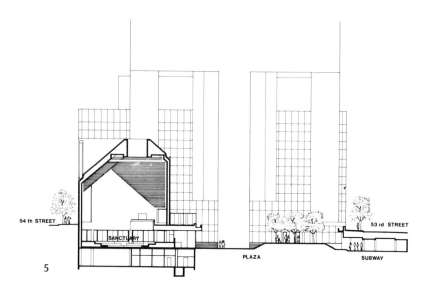

5

I made an early decision to place the great sanctuary space one level below grade, where it could gain additional area by extending beneath the pavements, where its large pipe organ could be accommodated, and where it would relate directly to the plaza space with its direct link to the subway entrances. This in turn led to the idea of a soaring superstructure above the sanctuary—pierced by skylight and windows and spanned by an entrance gallery. The diagonal thrust of the skylight in relation to the bank tower and the granite, prismatic form establish a dramatic but friendly confrontation with the smooth metal and glass facade of the tower. The church—basically a cube—is cut and shaped to give a strongly sculptural impression. Inside, walls rising 85 feet from the floor will be painted white, with natural wood on the large and important angled roof planes.

The entrance gallery—running parallel with the office building entry bridge—crosses the sanctuary and leads to an overlook where one can envision the entire space, and then on to a skylit chapel, and on again to the narthex, where broad stairs descend to the sanctuary below. From the gallery, deliberate and casual strollers will gain intriguing views into the life of the church at the intersection.

At street level the church also contains some rentable space, a bookstore, and other facilities. At the concourse level the sanctuary connects with the plaza and with a spacious and informal living room and library, flanked by offices for the clergy. Theater, workshops, choir, and lecture rooms occupy the full basement level. Additional offices, classrooms, and a day care center are placed on the second and third levels, which are integrated with the terraced, low-rise structure.

If religious experience is personal and mystical, it is also social and communal. In the words of the pastor, Ralph Edward Peterson, "Liturgy and worship of the Church is always drama, the original performing art." The sanctuary, originally large enough to accommodate 600 to 700 people, is therefore designed for performance. Acoustically treated, flanked by stepped seating, it can be a center for worship or for oratory, jazz evensong, choral or symphony concerts. When the church is not sponsoring these functions itself, it plans to lease the space as an auditorium.

Since, for the Lutheran, religious experience is personal as well as objective, the symbolism of the church is evocative and affirmative. The strong, granite forms, suggesting the rock on which New York is built, recall Christ's words to St. Peter, "Blessed art thou Simon called Peter, for on this rock shall I build my church."

6

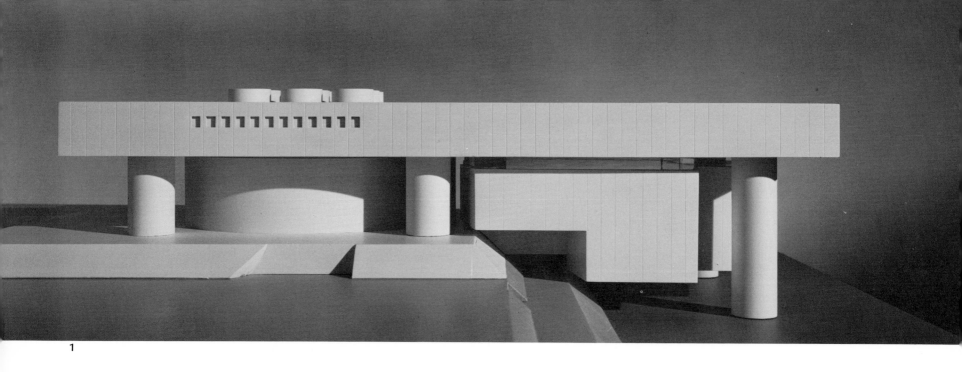

1

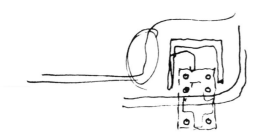

2

John F. Kennedy Library—Study for the University of Massachusetts, 1975

After 10 years of controversy over locating the John F. Kennedy Library in Cambridge, near Harvard University, it became clear that only the archive section of the library would be permitted in this location. The museum would have to be split away and located elsewhere.

The University of Massachusetts asked me to generate a design concept and study the feasibility of locating the entire library—archives and museum— on the University's Harbor Campus in Boston.

The concept embodies age-old motifs for memorials—the Pantheon and the Parthenon—brought into a single contemporary form. The great roof supported on six round supercolumns contains offices and archives. The museum, lecture hall, and rotunda are suspended from the trussed roof structure.

Sitting partially on an elevated plinth and partially over the water, the design embodies a sense of strength and dignity. It is a single entity, a total thing—expressing a feeling of permanence.

After numerous conferences and estimates, this concept was presented to the Kennedy Library Corporation some days before their meeting to evaluate the alternative locations. The Corporation selected the Harbor Campus Site.

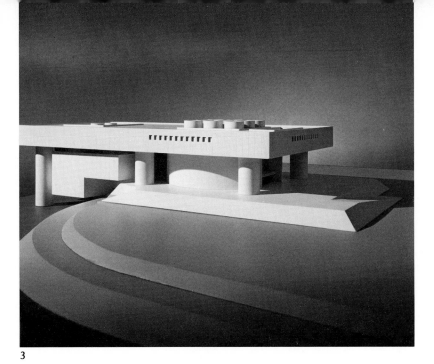

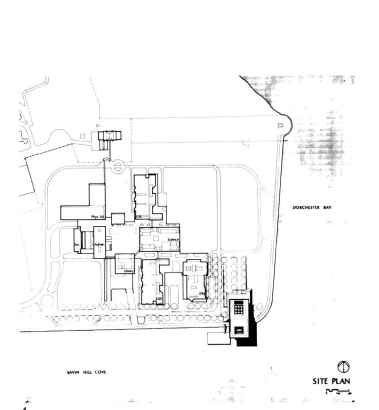

3

1 view of model from the west
2 original concept sketch by Hugh Stubbins
3 model from the northeast
4 site plan
5 principal floor plan
6 longitudinal section

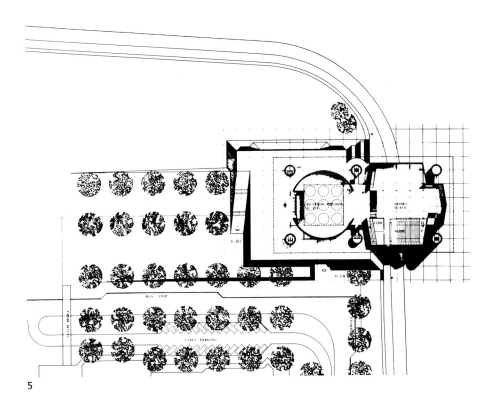

5

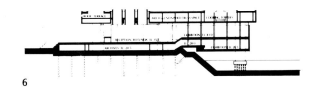

6

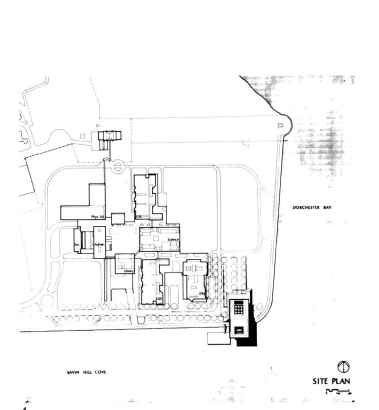

DORCHESTER BAY

SAVIN HILL COVE

SITE PLAN

4

175

Chronology

HUGH ASHER STUBBINS, JR., FAIA

January 11, 1912

Born in Birmingham, Alabama, eldest son of Hugh Asher and Lucile (Matthews) Stubbins

1933

Bachelor of Science in Architecture, Georgia Institute of Technology

1935

Master in Architecture, Harvard University

1935–1938

First job was in office of Royal Barry Wills, whose success in small house design had brought him national recognition and a Presidential medal. That year Richard Neutra had eclipsed Wills with his modern houses. Disarmingly aware of his limitation in this direction, Wills asked Stubbins to help him compete in modern design.

Stubbins remembers his association with Wills with great pleasure. While they were together, he designed and built six modern houses and won, jointly with Wills, several national design competitions, and designed an experimental trailer, unfortunately never produced.

1938–1939

Partnership with Marc Peter brought early national design recognition in the form of awards in national design competitions. Among the prize-winning schemes were: first prize, American Gas Association and *Architectural Forum* National House Competitions; third prize in the open competition for the Smithsonian Gallery of Art; fifth prize in the Williamsburg Competition sponsored by the *Architectural Record* and the National Academy of the Theatre; two prizes in *Ladies Home Journal* and *Architectural Forum* National House Competition; third prize in the U.S. National Competition for a post office in Covington, Kentucky.

Also designed the Telepix Cinema, Boston, and houses published in the *Christian Science Monitor*. Stubbins recalls that, at the end of the depression, there was very little work but that the competitions sponsored by magazines and manufacturing companies gave architects much needed publicity and quite valuable cash prizes. He is always grateful to the *Shelter* magazines for, to some extent, launching his career in residential design.

Married Diana Hamilton Moore (1938). Two sons of this marriage, Hugh III and Michael.

Returned to hometown of Birmingham (1939) to become chief designer in the firm of Miller, Martin, and Lewis.

1940

Two telegrams on the same day from Harvard changed the course of his career—one awarding him the Wheelwright Traveling Fellowship the other from Walter Gropius inviting him to come to Harvard as his assistant. Accepted Gropius' offer and postponed the fellowship. Moved to Cambridge, began teaching, and set up his first design office.

Designed 100-unit defense housing project at Windsor Locks, Connecticut. Houses were built for a unit cost of $2,500 and incorporated an experimental anthracite stove for heating, cooking, and hot water. Project cited by the Museum of Modern Art in New York as "one of the best 50 examples of architecture in 10 years." Friendship with Alvar Aalto and Marcel Breuer.

It was during this period that Stubbins, with other young architects—among them Sert, Breuer, Kahn, and Perkins—started the American Society of Planners and Architects (ASPA), a counterorganization to the AIA.

As Stubbins recalls, "It was a time when there was not much building to do. ASPA was launched at a big meeting in the Waldorf Astoria ballroom. Many subsequent meetings took place in Philadelphia and at LeBistro in New York. It never really got off the ground, and ASPA lasted about 3 years until business began to pick up and we didn't have time for it anymore."

Stubbins sees this as an exciting and formative period in his development as an architect. He developed a close bond with Alvar Aalto, whose work he probably admires above that of any living architect and whose influence on his own work he readily acknowledges.

1940–1945

Joined Harvard's Radio Research Laboratory and helped produce the machine afterward employed by the American Air Force to jam enemy radar. Collaborated with MIT professor John Rule in establishing the Stereographic Company to develop techniques for drawing three-dimensional pictures and slides used for training naval pilots and gunners. Also worked under Dr. Edwin Land of Polaroid who developed the so-called "educated bomb" based on a heat-homing device.

1946–1947

Became Associate Professor, Harvard Graduate School of Design. Designed and built his own house and office in Lexington, Massachusetts. Ulrich Franzen, Harry Cobb, Robert Geddes, John Myer, Fletcher Ashley, Frank Schlessinger, and I. M. Pei worked in his office during this time. The practice consisted mainly of private houses, many of which seem almost as modern today as when they were designed.

Having been something of a maverick in regard to organized professional associations, Stubbins finally became a member of the AIA in 1947.

1948

AIA national convention speaker at Salt Lake City. Received first public school commission, along with low-cost housing projects. The practice then developed a strong school specialty. Became visiting critic in residence in the Architectural Department of Yale University.

With Bob Little, Bob Elkington, John Carl Warnecke, Ralph Rapson, Ernest Kump, and others, founded the now celebrated "Egg and Dart Club." The initial idea of the club was a "back to first principles" forum for discussion to counteract the journal-sponsored social suites at the annual AIA conventions. The Egg and Dart Club has become an influential group; only the initiated and their invited guests are admitted at convention time.

1949

Hugh Stubbins and Associates founded with Stubbins as President. Listed for the first time in *Who's Who in America*.

1950–1951

Became visiting critic to the University of Oregon. Received AIA Award of Merit for the Adams Residence, Concord, Massachusetts.

Gave a series of lectures (1951) at the Georgia Institute of Technology.

1953

Following Gropius' resignation, became Chairman of the Department of Architecture, the Harvard Graduate School of Design, until 1954, when he, too, resigned to devote full time to a growing practice. He recalls his teaching experience as a time of great stimulus. Believing that design cannot really be taught, he tried to create within his studio an atmosphere that nurtured talent and allowed it to grow. Many of the men and

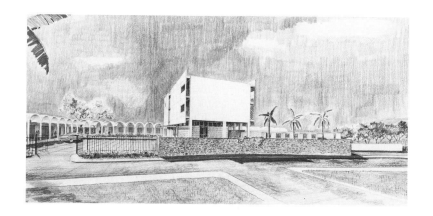

women who have since become influential in the profession passed through his studio at one time or another—among them, Philip Johnson, Wilhelm Von Moltke, Paul Rudolph, Victor Lundy, Ulrich Franzen, Henry Cobb, Robert Geddes, Bruno Zevi, Chip and Sarah Harkness, Mel Brecher, and others. There is both affection and admiration in his recollections of Walter Gropius. "Gropius with his broad vision and soft heart that made it impossible for him to fail a student; a design philosophy in many ways different from my own; but at times almost prophetic vision and a gift for philosophical communication that has to be called inspiring."

1954

Invited by the Architectural Advisory Committee of the Department of State to design the U.S. Consulate in Tangier, Morocco.

Received *Progressive Architecture* First Design Award for proposed Back Bay Center scheme for downtown Boston. The scheme was a collaboration among Stubbins, Gropius, Belluschi, Walter Bogner, and Carl Koch.

Elected Associate Member, National Academy of Design.

1955

Selected by the American Institute of Architects to design the Congress Hall, West Berlin, Germany.

Awarded Harleston Parker Gold Medal for the Country School, Weston, Massachusetts.

The period of design and construction of the Berlin Congress Hall was one of the high points of Stubbins' career; he says "there was so much hope and symbolism invested in the building . . . hope for peace, cooperation, progress in thought, humanity, and knowledge. The whole city of Berlin watched the development of the building with intense interest and nicknamed it the 'pregnant oyster' when they became aware of the design concept with the, at the time, daring and innovative catenary roof formation. People worked so hard in Berlin at that time . . . the building was completed in 15 months."

Der letzte Schrei

KONGRESSHALLE

„Na, Männe, bin ich nicht mit meinem neuen Früh-
jahrshut ganz ,up to date'?"   Zeichnung Stenzel

1956

One of eight American architects selected to enter a competition for the design of the American Embassy in London. (Eero Saarinen won the competition, and his building now stands in Grosvenor Square.)

1957

Elected Fellow of the American Academy of Arts and Sciences.

Berlin Congress Hall completed.

Hugh Stubbins and Associates incorporated in the Commonwealth of Massachusetts.

1958

Awarded Silver Medal of the Architectural League of New York for the Congress Hall, Berlin.

Became a member of the Visiting Committee, Harvard Graduate School of Design.

1960

Elected Fellow in Design of the American Institute of Architects.

Two United States architects invited by the World Health Organization to enter an international design competition for their headquarters in Geneva (Stubbins and Saarinen).

The Loeb Drama Center, Harvard, completed.

During the sixties, the Stubbins' office moved heavily into university architecture to meet the expanding student enrollment most colleges were experiencing at that time. Began a relationship with Mount Holyoke College that has lasted to the present day and has encompassed ten buildings.

His first marriage ended in divorce. Married Colette Fadeuilhe in September of this year.

1961

Awarded AIA "Award of Merit" for the Unitarian Church, Concord, Massachusetts.

Received Boston Arts Festival Award for the Loeb Drama Theatre, Harvard.

Received Rodgers and Hammerstein Award for the Loeb Drama Theatre, Harvard.

1962

Became a member of the Advisory Council to Princeton University School of Architecture.

First Mount Holyoke College Dormitory Building—1837 Hall—completed.

Maimonides School, Brookline, and the Beverly School for the Deaf completed.

1963

Married student housing at MIT completed.

Received "Boston Arts Festival Award" for the Maimonides School.

Progressive Architecture "Design Award" for the Senior Residences, the Dana Hall Schools, Wellesley, Massachusetts.

1964

Asked to serve on the Arts and Architecture Committee for the John F. Kennedy Memorial Library.

Chairman of the Design Advisory Committee of the Boston Redevelopment Authority.

Started 5-year term as Director of the Benjamin Franklin Foundation, Berlin, Germany.

Elected Vice President of the American Institute of Architects.

Bowdoin Senior Center completed.

Princeton dormitories and first University of Massachusetts dining commons completed.

Member of the AIA Pan American Congress Committee.

1965

Began 5-year term as first Chairman of the Selection Committee, Thomas Jefferson Memorial Chair, University of Virginia.

Francis A. Countway Library of Medicine, Harvard University, completed.

First University of Massachusetts dormitories completed.

1966

Received Awards of Merit from the American Institute of Architects and the American Library Association for the Countway Library of Medicine.

New England Regional Council of the American Institute of Architects gave Design Award to Hugh Stubbins and Associates, for Senior Residences, Dana Hall Schools.

Firm also received Award of Merit from the United States Office of Education for the Mathematics–Physics Complex, Princeton University.

Appointed executive architect for the Philadelphia Stadium.

Became member of Design Review Panel of the Worcester Redevelopment Authority.

Mount Holyoke College Laboratory Theater completed.

Moved to new house of his own design at 199 Brattle Street, Cambridge.

1967

American Institute of Architects presented "The Firm Award," to Hugh Stubbins and Associates, Inc., its highest award for an architectural firm, for "its consistent work of highest quality both in design and detailed execution. Its awareness of human needs and its sensitive respect for environment and tradition . . . inspiring to student and public alike."

Architectural Record Award of Excellence (Record Houses) for Brattle Street House.

Rochester Institute of Technology, College of Fine and Applied Arts and College of Graphic Arts and Photography Building completed.

Mount Holyoke, Ham and MacGregor Halls and Psychology and Education Building completed.

1968

Final completion of University of Massachusetts Southwest Quadrangle complex.

1969

Formed joint-venture partnership with Rex Allen for health facility work and became principal of Hugh Stubbins/Rex Allen partnership.

Hugh Stubbins and Associates, Inc., moved to a new building, developed and designed by the firm, at 1033 Massachusetts Avenue, Cambridge.

Vice President of Boston Society of Architects and Juror of the National Honor Award Program of the AIA.

Juror, American Library Association.

Warren Gardens Low-Income Housing, Roxbury, Massachusetts, completed, also University of California at Santa Cruz, College No. 5.

1970

Elected President of the Boston Society of Architects.

Director of Cambridge Chamber of Commerce.

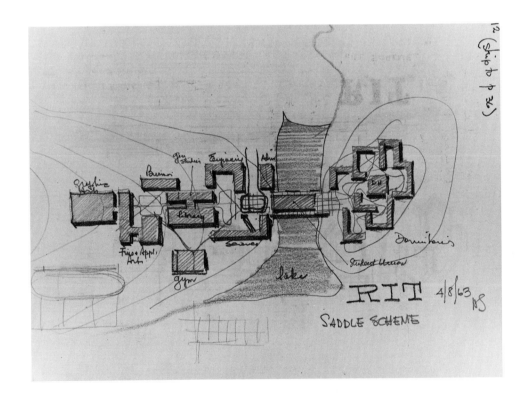

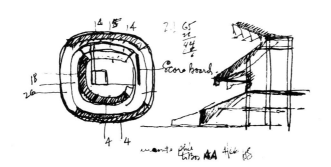

Juror in the sixth annual review of A T & T Bell Telephone Systems Buildings.

Awarded AIA Award of Merit for Warren Gardens Low-Income Housing.

Brandeis Student Union and Hampshire College Academic Building, Library, Dormitories, and Dining Complex completed.

Princeton Physics Building completed.

Appointed Member, United States Military Academy Planning Advisory Board.

1971

Became Secretary and Trustee of the Rotch Traveling Scholarship Committee and Juror, American Academy in Rome Prize.

Hugh Stubbins and Associates, Inc., received *Architectural Record* Award of Excellence for Warren Gardens Housing and Prestressed Concrete Institute Award for the Philadelphia Veterans Stadium.

Unionmutual Headquarters Building, Portland, Maine, completed.

Mount Holyoke College Art Building completed.

1972

Hugh Stubbins and Associates, awarded contract for the Federal Reserve Bank of Boston.

Member of Mayor's Panel of Architects, New York City.

Member, National Advisory Council, Hampshire College.

Firm also awarded AIA Collaborative Achievement Medal for the Colleges of Fine and Applied Art and Graphic Arts and Photography at the Rochester Institute of Technology.

Hugh Stubbins and Associates, Inc., awarded the College and University Conference and Exposition Citation for Excellence in Architecture for College No. 5, University of California at Santa Cruz.

Tabor Academy Academic Building completed, also MIT Graduate Student Housing, Westgate II.

1973

The firm moved into large-scale urban planning and architecture with the Federal Reserve Bank of Boston in working drawings and a contract for the huge Citicorp Center, New York City, for the First National City Bank. The firm also began studies for the speculative Spring Venture Development in Atlanta. Work started also on the Nathan Marsh Pusey Library for Harvard to be placed below grade to avoid disruption of the venerated Harvard Yard.

Member of the Harleston Parker Medal Committee.

"The Bank", Manchester, New Hampshire, completed; also completed, the Master's Residence and Dormitories at Tabor Academy.

Award of Merit, Institute of Southern Affairs and the Southern Academy of Letters, Arts, and Sciences.

1974–1975

Elected Academician, National Academy of Design, and Member of the AIA Jury of Fellows.

Elected Trustee of Tabor Academy.

Juror, 1974 Awards Program, Texas Society of Architects.

Honorary Fellow, Mexican Society of Architects (1974).

Chairman, AIA South Atlantic Region Awards Program.

American Association of School Administrators Citation (1974) Tabor Academy and (1975) Mount Wachusett Community College, Gardner, Massachusetts.

National Technical Institute for the Deaf at Rochester Institute of Technology completed and awarded Top Honors in the *American School and University* Awards Program.

Hewlett-Packard Medical Equipment Manufacturing Plant on Route 128, Boston, completed.

University of Virginia, School of Law, Graduate School of Business Administration, and Judge Advocate General's School completed.

Awarded Contract for Technical College in Shiraz, Iran.

Photograph Credits

Henderson Barr, 184 (middle)

Morley Baer, 140, 141

Lois M. Bowen, 154

Louis Checkman, 125

George F. Conley, 21, 23, 26, 46 (5), 160, 171, 173

Robert Damora, 57

Neil Doherty, 109 (3)

Charles Forberg, 56, 62, 63

Richard Garrison, 59, 64, 65, 178 (top)

Jonathan Green, 34, 35, 36 (8), 90, 91, 102, 103 (8), 104, 107, 108 (1), 122, 123, 136, 137, 146, 147, 150, 151, 157, 184 (top)

W. Easley Hamner, 43 (11), 170

Donald Hanson, 143 (3)

Robert D. Harvey, 31, 40, 88, 89 (5), 142, 143 (2)

Haskell, 176 (top)

David Hirsch, 180 (bottom)

Howard Associates, 18, 148

Hutchins Photography, 133, 134 (5)

Edward Jacoby, 78 (10), 82 (2), 185

Clemens Kalischer, 103 (7), 155

Phokion Karas, 36 (7), 37, 38, 43 (10), 48, 49, 134 (6)

Foto Kessler, 158–159, 163 (6, 8)

Ernest Kump, 178 (bottom)

Lynn McLaren, vi

Joseph W. Molitor, 72, 73, 94, 153

Gerald Ratto, 139

Louis Reens, 77 (5), 99 (9), 101, 110, 113, 114, 116, 117, 119, 120, 121, 134 (7), 181 (top)

Samuel Robbins, 16, 28, 29, 30, 42

Steve Rosenthal, 44, 47, 174 (1), 175 (3) 184 (bottom)

Gottscho Schleisner, 55

Robert Schwartz, 33

Skyviews, 19

Ezra Stoller, 53, 54, 60, 61, 68, 69, 75, 77 (6, 7, 8), 79, 84–85, 87, 97, 98 (4, 5), 111, 112, 124, 126, 127, 129, 131, 180 (top)

Hugh Stubbins, 24, 45, 50, 52, 58, 66, 74, 78 (9), 80, 86, 96, 100, 138, 174 (2), 176 (bottom) 177 (top) 179 (top), 182, 183

Hugh Stubbins III, 106

Lawrence S. Williams, 156

Foto Wimmer, 163 (7)

George Zimberg, 98 (3), 135, 144

Index